Spain

Spain

Authentic regional recipes

M. Teresa Segura

CHARTWELL
BOOKS, INC.

This edition published in 2011 by
Chartwell Books, Inc.
A division of Book Sales, Inc.
276 Fifth Avenue Suite 206
New York, New York 10001
USA

QTT.WFSP

A Quintet Book
Copyright © Quintet Publishing Limited

Cover photo © Garlick, Ian / Stockfood America

ISBN-13: 978-0-7858-2872-3

Project Editor: Robert Davies
Designer: Rod Teasdale
Art Director: Michael Charles
Managing Editor: Donna Gregory
Publisher: Mark Searle
Additional Text: Camilla Barton, Diana Craig

This book was conceived, designed, and produced by
Quintet Publishing Limited
The Old Brewery
6 Blundell Street
London N7 9BH
United Kingdom

Printed and bound in Singapore

10 9 8 7 6 5 4 3 2 1

Contents

Introduction

Spanish food is fresh, healthy, flavorful, and uncomplicated, and is based on the produce which is grown and sold locally. This cuisine is the perfect match for modern tastes, which lean toward simple food with bold flavors. This book introduces a range of Spanish flavors, from the classic tapas dishes popular in bars across the country to more sophisticated dishes which show off the finest produce of the different regions. Many of these recipes are prepared using the same ingredients and techniques as were used centuries ago; others show the recent influence of wider European and American cooking on Spanish food. What these 100 recipes have in common is their freshness, simplicity, and fine flavors.

Taberna La Ardosa, Madrid.

The regions of Spain

Though its borders are clearly defined, Spain has been a single country for fewer than 500 years—so it is unsurprising that each region is more conscious of its individual identity than of its Spanish nationality. Food is a prominent way in which the regions express their local identities. The mountain ranges which run across the peninsula have played a large part in making the food of each community distinct from that enjoyed by neighboring regions—especially because, until the last half of the twentieth century, transportation between the regions was difficult.

There are, though, themes which run through the cooking of the whole country and which make it possible to speak of a distinctively Spanish style of cooking. The Moors, who stayed for nearly a millennium, influenced the cooking of the south of Iberia, in particular, and the ingredients they introduced remain popular.

The struggle to throw out the infidels brought a second influence to Spanish food. Because Muslims do not eat pork, this meat became a key ingredient and the cooking of pork was elevated to a position of real respect in Christian Spanish society.

A third common idea is the respect for and interest in fine ingredients. Many countries claim to produce the finest foods in Europe, but Spain is a strong contender. Its harvests of olives, citrus fruits, peppers, and rice are of an extremely high standard. Wine- and sherry-making are crafts which have long been cultivated. Spanish cooks are extremely skilled at devising simple recipes designed to show off their food without unnecessary complications. The recipes in this book all derive from this centuries-old tradition. The food featured here, and the food enjoyed across Spain, may be straightforward—but it is extremely tasty.

Houses by the coast in Cudillero—a fishing village in Asturias, on the ancient route of pilgrimage called the Way of Saint James.

The North (Galicia, Asturias, Cantabria)

Northern Spain has a climate and landscape far different from that of the beaches in the south—and this is reflected in the local food. The coast is buffeted by strong Atlantic winds and queimada is its antidote. This punch is made from Galician aguardiente—a spirit distilled from wine and flavored with herbs or coffee, plus sugar, lemon peel, coffee beans, and cinnamon. Fantastic fish stews are made here, as the north coast provides some of the best shellfish and seafood in Europe, including octopus, oysters, huge orange mussels, scallops, and rock lobsters.

Galicia, the north-west corner of Spain, has a Celtic heritage, bagpipe music, a rainy climate, and rugged coastlines. The region supplies the whole of Spain with cabbages, turnips, and potatoes. The best-known dishes are broths with cabbage, like caldo gallego, and lacon con grelos, a ham knuckle with young turnip tops. Unique to the area are empanadas—flat pies filled with shellfish, sardines, or pork and bell peppers. An almond tart is a Galician speciality made to celebrate Saint James's Day. Local recipes rarely include olive oil or garlic. In the hillier but poorer south, chestnut trees are prolific and chestnuts are eaten like potatoes are elsewhere.

To the east of Galicia lies Asturias, a region noted for its wild forests. Known for producing the best milk in Spain, Asturias is home to the famous cabrales, a blue-vein cheese aged in natural caves in the limestone mountains of the area. There are over two dozen varieties of cow, sheep, and goat's milk cheeses.

This area is home to many varieties of apple, used to fill warm apple pies and make strong, fizzy cider. Being a European wilderness, pigeon, partridge, red deer, trout, and salmon are found in abundance.

A popular destination for Spanish family holidays, the Cantabrian coast to the east of Asturias boasts excellent seafood. This lush, green province is known for its fine dairy products and cheese-based desserts such as quesada pasiega. Away from the coast, the climate favors cattle-breeding and dishes focus on meat, which is broiled or stewed. Beef, ox, deer, roe deer, or boar are used. Typical main meals are cocido montañés (Highlander stew) made with beans, meat, cabbage, and potato, and cocido lebaniego (Liébanan stew) made with meat and garbanzo beans.

The Pyrenees (Navarre, Basque Country, Aragon)

The Basque country in north-east Spain has a long tradition of cooking, and its people are considered Spain's most fervent chefs, with recipes handed down generations and gastronomic societies everywhere. Being next to both the Bay of Biscay and the mountains that lead to France, there are several different styles and the meals often reflect a French influence. Traditional Basque cuisine focuses on seafood, especially the salt cod, which is often cooked in a peppery sauce. Hake, sole, spider crab, baby eels, line-caught squid, and shellfish also dominate. Some more unusual delicacies are fresh hake cheeks, wild boar, sea urchins, and calves' snouts and brains. The mountains provide fine meat and game, dairy products, vegetables, and wild mushrooms. Flavorful sauces are made with herbs, tomatoes, and bell peppers. Chocolate is a local passion and txakoli is a light wine perfect with seafood.

Navarre, to the east, enjoys a temperate climate with mountains and green valleys in the north and dusty plains in the south. The region is the largest tomato producer in Spain and the description "a la Navarra" means "with tomatoes." One classic dish from Navarre involves pan-frying mountain-stream trout with cured ham inserted and served on a bed of tomatoes and onions. Lovely vegetables are cultivated in the warm Ebro valley and often cooked in a vegetable stew "menestre." Tudela is famous for its asparagus which is made into tortillas, and pointed spicy red peppers are best from Lodoso. These pimientos del pico are stuffed with meat or salt cod to make a delicious meal. Wheat, corn, and vineyards that bottle popular wines are also found here. High in the mountains, lambs are reared for dishes like cochifrito and chilindron, wild rabbits are stewed with snails and herbs, and pigeons are netted to add to a raisin and pine nut sauce.

Aragon is a large, wealthy region with five climate zones and contrasting landscapes. The Pyrenees tower in the north and Ebro, the largest volume river in Spain, crosses Aragon from west to east. Perfect conditions in northern areas provide green meadows for lamb and beef breeding and the upper river valleys provide trout, salmon, boar, truffles, and mushrooms to the region. The lower irrigated areas grow expanses of wheat, barley, rye, fruit, and grapes for wine. Terul's famous ham is delicious cooked with red bell peppers al chilindron. A traditional dish of salt cod flavored with red bell peppers is enjoyed here, as well as other seafood combinations such as crab paste.

Benasque—a small town nestling in the heart of the Pyrenees.

Catalonia

The best and freshest food in Barcelona is to be found in markets like this one, where a huge array of Iberian foodstuffs are sold.

Catalonia in the north-east boasts the most sophisticated Spanish regional cuisine, most likely due to the combination of mountain and coastal locales and the common border with France. The capital Barcelona has enjoyed a reputation for over 150 years as a city of good eating. Spain's alternative to champagne, called cava, is produced in Sant Sadurní d'Anoia, nearby.

Adventurous pairings like lobster and chicken, lobster and chocolate sauce, and goslings with figs are common in Catalonia. Zarzuela and suquet—gorgeous fish stews—are the highlights on this region's menu. Other stews include beans with the local fat white sausage called butifarra—made of pork and spices. Various Catalan sauces enrich the meat and seafood flavors, including allioli, romesco, picada, and samfaina. Bacalao con samfaina pairs salt cod with a tomato, bell pepper, and eggplant sauce, and grilled seafood is delicious with the chile and hazelnut romesco sauce. All meals come with tomato-coated bread, pan con tomate. Creamy desserts, like curds with honey and the local crème brûlée, crema Catalana, are popular.

While there are many popular rice dishes here, pasta such as cannelloni is sometimes used. A traditional lobster dish, called rossejat de fideos, resembles paella but instead of rice, it has fideos—fine vermicelli-like pasta. Catalans celebrate both the hunting and eating of local mushrooms, particularly rovellos, during the mushroom festival in the fall. The prized pickings are showed off to the townspeople and then the mushrooms are lovingly sautéed in olive oil and garlic, and garnished with parsley.

The East (Murcia, Valencia, the Balearic Islands)

Murcia, a small region of south-eastern Spain, is by no means small in the way of culinary offerings. Home of several excellent wineries and delicately flavored rice from Calasparra, the region boasts top-quality products that go into and accompany its food. Local rice dishes include arroz con conejo y caracoles—rice with rabbit and snails—and other combinations of vegetables, chicken, or beans. Irrigation systems put in place by the Moors centuries ago help to keep the region producing vast quantities of fresh fruits, vegetables, and flowers. Murcian specialties include the omelet-style zarangollo—tomato, zucchini, onion, and egg—and the small pasty pastel de carne, filled with meat, tomatoes, and egg. Mar Menor, a salty lagoon on the coast of Murcia, provides wonderful fish and shellfish, used in a variety of ways. There's the fish soup sopa de pescado and salty fish such as the roe huevas, pescadoa a la sal—typically bass or gray mullet baked in salt, and escabeche— fished baked in oil and vinegar.

Valencia, east of Murcia, is a sharp contrast to its neighbor. While Murcia is one of the hottest and driest territories in Europe, Valencia occupies fertile land called the huerta. Orange, lemon, and peach groves abound and rice fields, also harboring eels, cover the farmland. Rice is made into paella or cooked in a fish broth and served with allioli. Eels are popular and cooked with garlic and paprika. In the summer, the ice-cold milky drink horchata is served, made from tigernuts, water, and sugar.

The Balearic Islands off the eastern coast—including Majorca, Minorca, Ibiza, and Formentera—have a long history of various cultures sweeping over them, which have all contributed to the area's food. Fresh fish is often on the menu, such as rock lobster which is cooked with herb-flavored spirits, and the fish stew zarzuela. Solid peasant vegetable dishes like oliagua soups and tumbet also feature as well as the local paprika and blood sausage sobrasada. The sausage is used in sofrit pages—an island stew of gently spiced pork, lamb, chicken, bell peppers, potatoes, and a rich aromatic juice. Excellent pizzas called coca are made here with four main varieties: sweet, savoury, closed and open. Mayonnaise originated in Minorca, although the French left the islands after occupation in the 1770s and took it as their own. The English around this time left behind their gin, which is still widely drunk on the islands today. Ibizan desserts such as the almond cake gato d'Ametlla and the cheesecake flao are both popular. However, the light pastry ensaimada is the island's treasure—similar to a croissant, filled with chocolate or cream, or eaten plain with sugar.

Valencia is famed for its combination of a rich architectural, culinary, and cultural history with a cutting-edge approach to design, food, and nightlife.

The Parque del Buen Retiro in Madrid is a popular place for the city's inhabitants to relax.

Central and Western Spain (Castile, La Mancha, Madrid, Extremadura)

Due to its central location, Madrid was given the role of Spain's capital 400 years ago. The city's inhabitants enjoy their meat, including thick steaks and milk-fed veal from Avila. Cocido madrileño is one of Spain's national dishes from here—a vast cauldron of meats, vegetables, garbanzo beans, and herbs that simmer all day to create this meal. Tapas bars are plentiful for tourists and residents alike, with complimentary hot or cold tastings of the tuna delicacy mojama, potato omelet tortilla de patata, shrimps gambas and the Spanish ham jamón among many others.

The interior of Spain is defined by countryside cuisine with heart-warming stews and roasts of lamb, suckling pig cochinillo, and goat cooked in old Arab beehive ovens. The cold air on the high plateau during winter is perfect for curing various meats and cheeses, such as cured sheep's cheese queso manchego. Castile and Leon (unified in 1983), north of Madrid over the Guadarrama mountains, is sometimes referred to as Spain's breadbasket—fine wheat is grown here and turned into large, round white loaves. Small areas have their own specialties like Sepulveda's suckling lamb, the tiny roast piglets of Arevolo, and the sweet yellow cakes of Avila. The poorer families of Castile and Leon eat beans, lentils, and garbanzo beans, as in the tasty garbanzos con chorizos.

South of Madrid is Castile La Mancha, known for sunflowers, olive groves, windmills, and Don Quixote. Manchego cheese originates here, as well as the tortilla. The hard climate of bitterly cold winters and harsh summers, have bred strong, raw tastes. Common foods include garlic soups, meatballs, chickpeas, and dishes with thyme and cumin. These flavorings arrived with the Arabs who also planted saffron, which is now thought to be the finest in the world. Pisto Manchego is a blend of tomatoes and vegetables served either hot or cold, as a main or starter. Partridges are used to make pâté, or cooked with wine and vinegar.

Andalusia

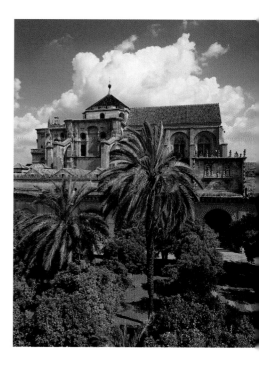

The Mezquita in Cordoba is a Roman Catholic cathedral but the structure was formerly the world's second-largest mosque.

Andalusia is perhaps the epitome of all things the tourist thinks of as typically Spanish—sangria, bullfighting, flamenco dancing, olive groves, and orange trees. It covers one-sixth of the country and has five coastal provinces, with sunny tourist beaches along the coast. In contrast, the high mountains of Grenada have cold winters and host skiing until May. Seafood is prevalent in Andalusia with fried fish pescaito frito from Cadiz a specialty. Along the Costa del Sol are sold battered squid rings calamares, excellent fish soups, stews of shark, skate cooked with paprika, and broiled swordfish steaks.

Various cultural groups have influenced the food found here today. The Islamic influence from the Moorish occupation is still strong, in the presence of cumin, saffron, ground nuts, and the planting of the olive and orange trees. Chilled soups, barbecued skewered meat, quince paste membrillo, and their way of pickling meat continues from the past. Another group to influence the cuisine were the gypsies—stews of beans, vegetables, and fruit, and dishes of tripe with sausage and garbanzo beans remain. Perhaps the most colorful gypsy dish, huevos flamencos, is a mixture of eggs, bell peppers, shrimp, and sausages. Andalusia was the first to bring American foods like corn, tomatoes, bell peppers, and potatoes to Europe and Seville is famous for introducing oranges—including the dish duck with orange.

Raw ham with bread is a popular tapa here. These hams can be seen hanging over bars and are cured in the cold sierra air, giving them the name serrano. The best known of these is jabugo ham. Other traditional Andalusian dishes include the cold vegetable soup gazpacho, bull's tail rabo de toro, and delicate dishes of veal.

Various convents in the capital Seville are still making a variety of lovely sweet pastries—a tradition dating back to medieval times. These include yemas, made from egg yolk and sugar, and rosquillas rellenas de cidra—cider pastries.

The area around Jerez produces the world's finest sherry. The dry and pale sherry fino is well paired chilled with fish and also used in cooking sauces.

Key ingredients of the Spanish kitchen

It was Spanish explorers in Mexico who introduced the chile pepper to Europe and thence to Asia.

Before the days of supermarkets and the mass transportation of food, cooks had to make use of local produce, and this varied depending on local climate. In Spain, for example, the raw ingredients available in the wet and windy north–west coastal region differed from those on offer in hot, dry Andalusia in the south, and this resulted in regional cuisines with their own distinct character. Several mountain ranges dissect the country, too, making transportation and communication more difficult and reinforcing historical regional differences. Foods introduced by invaders, such as the Romans and Moors, or brought back from the New World, further enriched Spain's culinary melting pot.

It is hard to give a shortlist of those ingredients that typify Spanish cuisine across the regions, but the following are just some of the key foodstuffs. The two items that most characterize Spanish cooking are olive oil and garlic—a Roman legacy. Olive oil is used widely in cooking, in marinades and dressings, while the pungent tang of garlic spices many a savory dish.

Like garlic, onions are essential in Spanish cooking for the tangy flavor they impart to cooked dishes or to salads. Two other vegetables, potatoes and tomatoes—both gifts from the New World—feature in some of Spain's most famous dishes. Potatoes are a key ingredient in tortilla Española, or Spanish omelet, and in the well-known tapa, patatas bravas. Tomatoes are used in sauces and salads, and in Andalusia's famous gazpacho, a cold tomato soup. Eggs are another essential. As well as tortilla Española, they are used in a variety of omelets or baked in such dishes as huevos flamencos.

A cornerstone of traditional Spanish gastronomy, Serrano ham is cured for at least a year up in the mountains, then served in wafer-thin slices with such accompaniments as broad beans in habas con jamôn. Fish and seafood, including squid, shrimp, fresh anchovies, fresh sardines, and cod, are popular ingredients too—which is not surprising given that Spain has a total of 3,084 miles (4,964 km) of coastline allowing access to both the Mediterranean and Atlantic. Mojama, a type of air-cured tuna and a legacy of the early Arab invaders, is another fishy delicacy.

No discussion of the food of Spain would be complete without a mention of rice, introduced by the Moors who once occupied Spain. This grain forms the basis of what is probably the most famous Spanish dish of all, paella, as well as other lesser-known recipes. Saffron—another ingredient from Spain's Moorish legacy—is the spice that gives paella rice its characteristic yellow coloring.

Parsley—the flat-leaved variety—is probably the most popular herb. Oregano, thyme, and rosemary are used too. Pimenton, Spanish paprika, is a storecupboard essential. It is a characteristic flavoring of chorizo, the spicy sausage made of coarsely chopped pork.

What pasta is to the Italians, bread is to the Spanish. The French-style bread stick known as a barra is served with every meal. It also makes its appearance with tapas and with the merienda, or afternoon snack. To many Spaniards, a meal is not complete without barra.

Olives have been cultivated in Spain for many centuries, and the country is now the world's largest producer. Notable varieties include the small brown Arbequina, which is excellent for eating, and the Manzanillo—a high-yielding variety which is very widely grown.

Techniques and equipment used in Spanish cooking

A well-equipped modern kitchen should meet most of the needs of anyone wanting to cook Spanish food. However, there are some more specialist pieces of equipment which can be added if liked, and which will give a more authentic feel.

The one dish that could be said to characterize Spanish cuisine is the stew known variously according to region as cocido, pote, guiso, estofado, escudella, or olla. Olla is also the name for the large casserole dish, wide in the middle and narrow at the top and bottom, which is a classic Spanish cooking utensil.

As well as concocting delicious stews, Spanish cooks also roast, fry, and sauté food. Traditionally, the classic Castilian lamb—spread with lard and sprinkled with water—is roasted in a clay dish, but a good set of roasting tins should suffice for most meats. Sturdy, heavy-bottomed (or non-stick) frying pans are essential for cooking tortilla Española and other types of omelet, while a deep fryer can be useful for various tapas, such as Andalucia's pescaditos—anchovies and other tiny fish which are coated in batter, then deep-fried—or deep-fried churros which are similar to doughnuts.

Although baking and broiling are not common, the Spaniards do broil meats on a metal plate or cook them over charcoal or an open fire. Available in a variety of materials, the olla—for cooking stews—can also be used over an open fire, as can the earthenware dish known as the cazuela. Available in a wide range of different sizes and infinitely adaptable, it can be placed in the oven, on the hob, on the barbecue, or over an open flame, and—conveniently—it retains its heat after cooking.

Another favorite barbecued food is sardines. Skewered and broiled over a fire, they are sold along the beachfronts on the Costa del Sol. In Catalonia, the dish known as calçotada—made from calocats, a type of scallion cooked over an open flame—symbolizes the coming of spring. Traditionally, the scallions are served on a terracotta roof tile, which keeps them warm. Another dish once cooked over an open fire is Valencia's famous paella. The essential piece of cookware for this is, of course, the round, shallow paellero, or paella pan, in which fideua, a paella made with noodles and fish stock, is also prepared.

Sardines grilling on a Spanish beach.

Every kitchen needs a good selection of knives, but when it comes to carving a Serrano ham, specialist equipment is pretty much essential in what amounts almost to a culinary ritual. A jamônero, or rack, holds the ham in place while it is carved using three razor-sharp knives—a culchillo de jamôn (a special long, flexible knife), a boning knife, and a wide-bladed cook's knife.

The mortar and pestle once used for pounding garlic or reducing the ingredients of gazpacho to a purée can, in the modern kitchen, be replaced by the more convenient garlic crusher and blender. A cook's blowtorch or, failing that, the grill, can be used to caramelize the thin, crackly sugar topping of crema Catalaña—Catalonia's version of crème brûlée—instead of the traditional hot iron.

Finally, a small, specially shaped bottle for drizzling olive oil makes a nice touch on the table. As the Spanish say to wish everyone a good meal: buen provecho.

TAPAS

BRAVAS	2.50
CALAMARES	3
SEPIA	2.50
PUNTILLA	3
CROQUETAS	0.50
TELLINAS	3
GAMBAS	4.50
ENSALADILLA	2
JAMON	5
BOQUERONES	2
QUESO	3
TORTILLA	2
CHAMPIÑON	2
PULPO	3

The culture of tapas

Eating tapas is as much part of the Spanish way of life as the traditional siesta. Ranging from simple finger foods like olives or toasted almonds to such cooked dishes as patatas bravas (potatoes in spicy sauce) or tortilla española (Spanish omelet), tapas are snacks taken before the main midday or evening meal. But these delicious appetizers offer a richer experience than the mere consumption of food. They are at the heart of an age-old cultural and social custom that reveals much about the Spanish approach to living, and that even has its own vocabulary. The tapeo is the name for the entire activity that surrounds the eating of tapas, while the verb tapear means "to go out and eat tapas."

The tapeo begins when Spaniards head for the bars known as tascas (tapas are not served in restaurants or at home). Here they gather to enjoy the company of family and friends, to chat, to gossip, to share a joke, and to debate the merits of the local soccor team or the state of the nation, while drinking and snacking. With a glass of wine or sherry (or cider in the north–west) in one hand and a tapa in the other, they build up an appetite for the meal to come—which in the evening can be as late as 10pm—or perhaps even eat so much that they need no further food. The tapeo is very much a moveable feast and participants often stroll from one bar to another. All are welcome to join in, including children.

The credit for the invention of the tapa is usually given to Alfonso X (1221–1284), el Sabio or "The Wise," ruler of Castile. Once, so the story goes, the king fell ill and during his illness had to take small quantities of food with a little wine between meals, presumably to keep up his strength. On his recovery, he decreed that forthwith wine should never be served in taverns unless accompanied by a snack. His intention was to protect the poor, who could not afford a meal with their wine and so became inebriated when drinking.

There are stories to explain the origin of the name "tapa" too. After Alfonso's decree was established, tavern-keepers are said to have served wine covered with a slice of smoked ham, cheese, or bread. This "tapa," meaning "lid" or "cover," was both an edible accompaniment to the drink and a way of keeping it free of the dirt, dust, or insects that might otherwise fall in.

Another variation on the tale again involves Alfonso X. During a journey through the province of Cádiz, he stopped off at the town of Ventorillo del Chato, where he ordered some sherry, the local fortified wine. Because it was windy, the landlord of the inn covered the royal drink with a slice of ham to protect it from wind-blown dirt. According to the story, the king was so appreciative that when he ordered a second glass, he asked for it to be covered with the same "tapa" as before.

A more down-to-earth explanation suggests that tapas were invented because farm and other manual workers needed to eat a little during their working hours to keep them going until their proper mealtimes arrived.

Gazpacho, paella, sangria: iconic dishes and drinks

Classic sangria.

Gazpacho

Gazpacho is a chilled, hearty soup, often thought of as a "liquid salad," only to be found during Spain's summer months. Gazpacho originates in Andalusia, and was originally a combination of stale bread, garlic, olive oil, salt, and vinegar. During the Middle Ages, Spanish farmers and shepherds were next to throw ripe vegetables into the mix to become a more satisfying meal. After Spain's discovery of the New World, tomatoes and bell peppers were added to make the gazpacho we know today.

This gradual addition of ingredients and the nature of the dish is reflected in its name. Gazpacho is believed by many to be derived from the word caspa meaning "fragments" or "leftovers." Indeed, there is no single recipe for gazpacho, as Spanish chefs will enthusiastically prepare the tasty soup with whatever vegetable they desire or have to hand. Traditionally, gazpacho was made with a mortar and the ingredients pounded to a paste. Today, blenders take out a lot of the hard work.

Paella

The most notable Spanish dish, the paella, began as a poor man's dish in the eighteenth century and rose to popularity outside of Valencia in the nineteenth century. The Romans introduced the round, shallow, steel pan which was later used to create the dish and the name is derived from the Latin word for pan, patella. The Moors brought rice and saffron to Valencia around this time and the peasants combined these with any other ingredient they could find. Traditionally it included land snails, chicken, rabbit, and seasonal vegetables. A later variation saw the addition of seafood and shellfish to paella. After stir-frying meat and vegetables in olive oil, short-grain rice such as calasparra and bomba is spread over the pan in a thin layer and soaks up all the flavors. A previously made broth is added before simmering and finally seasoning. The way to eat paella is communally from the pan, with the dish set in the middle of the table to share joyously with friends and family.

Paella valenciana.

Sangria

The light, summer wine punch known as sangría was created to refresh Spain's thirsty bar patrons and is thought of more as a party drink by locals. Originally, just made up of red wine and soda water, it was soon combined with chopped fruit, juice, and spirits such as brandy or triple sec to make it more appealing. The quality of the punch depends on the freshness of the fruit and flavours of the juice used. Although sangría can sometimes be made with white wine, with various alcoholic potencies, and no fixed recipe, it is always easy to drink and served ice-cold from a pitcher or punch bowl. Today, sangría can be found in almost every bar throughout Spain.

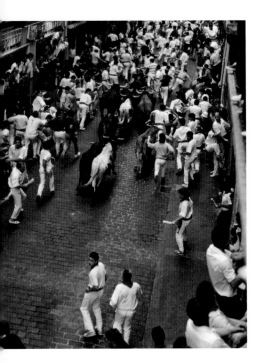

The festival of San Fermin, in the Navarrese city of Pamplona, is famous for its bull-running through the streets of the town.

Food and festivals

The best times to be had in Spain are at the many fiestas throughout the year—commemorating patron saints, historic battles, religious holidays, and the food itself. Depending on the location and celebration, various treats and feasts will be had by all.

Often cooking competitions provide the food to keep the revellers going throughout the festivities. On the eve of La Tomatina (the world's biggest tomato fight) in Buñol, the town's best cooks hold an unofficial paella contest, and during the Fiesta del Arroz (festival of rice) in Sueca, the competition becomes international. Pans of paella are cooked on the streets of Las Fallas (festival of fire) in Valencia to feed the crowds amidst fireworks and flames. During Aste Nagusia (big week) in Bilbao, when the town celebrates its Basque heritage, local chefs compete to produce the best hake in green sauce and cod in garlic sauce. The popular local drink kalimotxo (red wine and coke) is also consumed in large quantities.

At the well-known carnival in Pamplona—the Running of the Bulls—chorizo sausage, Spanish tortilla, thick beef stew, and jugs of red wine are all on offer. Chunks of thick country bread help to soak up all the wine. To celebrate the patron saint Virgin Del Rocio of Almonte, snacks of tortilla, jamón, shrimp, and fried bell peppers are handed out to the countryside campers and carnival goers over several days. There's also plenty of local wine and sherry to go around. Pungent octopus cooked in copper cauldrons can be found at the honor of the patron saint of resurrection, in the small town of Las Nieves. On the Monday following Easter, a huge picnic occurs on the banks of River Tormes, where friends and family gather to eat hornazo—a pastry pie filled with ham, sausage, bacon, cooked egg, and sometimes chicken.

Particular foods are the sole reason for many Spanish fiestas. Among those celebrated are artichokes in Benicaró, sausages in Requena, cherries in Serra, and potatoes and black truffles (on separate days) in Zorita del Maestrazgo. Viver's olive oil festival in Parque de la Floresta features more than 50 of the best oil producers in the region. Requena's grape harvest festival and Jerez's sherry festival are the fiestas for wine lovers. Jerez celebrates the grapes and blessing of the wine—100 varieties of which are available for tasting. O Grove holds the seafood festival where tasting of all fish–related dishes is encouraged. Calçotada is the occasion in Valls when massive amounts of calçots (scallions) are roasted and dipped in salvitxada or romesco sauce, and consumed with red wine or cava.

Fireworks during the Ferias festival, Salamanca.

Christmas Eve is the biggest meal of the year in Spain and families eat very well. Usually there will be lobster, roast lamb or suckling pig, fish soup, and a wealth of seafood, cheeses, hams, and pâtés. A variety of Christmas sweets may follow such as nougats (turron and jijona), marzipans (yema), and crumbly cakes (polvorones and mantecados). Another treat is rosquilloes de vino—cookies flavored with anise and wine. No Christmas plate would be complete without walnuts, dates, and mandarins. At the pagan festival on Christmas Eve in Baga, Catalonia, locals eat savory cake (coca) with garlic mayonnaise.

CHAPTER 1

Classic Dishes

Asturias
Galicia
Basque
Navarre
La Rioja
Castilla y Leon
Aragon
Catalonia
Costa Brava
Costa Dorado
MADRID
Costa del Azahar
Extremadura
Castilla La Mancha
Valencia
Balearic Islands
Murcia
Costa Blanca
Andalusia
Costa del Sol

Although Spanish cuisine has a strongly regional quality, the favorite ingredients and cooking techniques are shared across the country, meaning that some dishes have entered a classic repertoire of common foods. These are often straightforward tapas such as salads and grilled fish, and dishes based around the staple foods such as breads, legumes, and grains. Many desserts, too, fall into this category—regional variation is less pronounced here, with many classic desserts being based around milk, rice, and flavorings such as orange, cinnamon, and vanilla.

A matador in traditionally ornate dress prepares for a bullfight in Plaza de Toros de Ronda. It is a common misconception that the color red is supposed to anger the bull—bulls are actually colorblind.

Tortilla española
Spanish potato omelet

Ingredients
2 large potatoes
1 large onion
3 tbsp olive oil
2 cloves garlic, crushed
1 tsp dried oregano
1 bay leaf
6 large eggs
few drops Tabasco sauce (optional)
salt and freshly ground black pepper
chopped fresh parsley

Serves 6

*S*erved hot or cold, this simple Spanish dish of eggs, onion, and potato is a pleasure to eat. Sprinkle with fresh parsley and accompany with some crusty bread and a salad for lunch, or serve up with a piece of toast and coffee for breakfast.

Peel and cut the potatoes into small cubes about ¼ inch (5 mm) thick. Slice the onion into thin shreds.

Heat the oil in a large non-stick skillet and stir-fry the potatoes, onion, garlic, and oregano with the bay leaf over a high heat for 5 minutes. Reduce the heat and cook for about 20 minutes, stirring occasionally, taking care not to over brown the mixture.

Meanwhile, whisk together the eggs, Tabasco, if using, and plenty of seasoning.

Transfer the potato mixture into a 10-inch nonstick skillet, discard the bay leaf, and pour in the beaten eggs. Over a low heat, and stirring the set egg from the edge of the pan inward, cook the mixture for 5 minutes until all the runny egg has begun to set. Pack the mixture down well and continue to cook for a further 5 minutes.

Slide the tortilla on to a plate and return to the skillet the other way up. Cook gently for a further 5 minutes until set all the way through and golden brown. Serve hot or cold, cut into wedges and sprinkled with the parsley.

Tortilla de guisantes
Green pea tortilla

*T*his variation on the basic tortilla is excellent served in bite-size pieces with drinks.

Heat the oil in a 9-inch nonstick skillet. Add the onion, sprinkle with salt, and fry gently for about 25 minutes, until tender. Season to taste, then stir in the peas.

Beat the eggs with the mint, and salt and pepper, then pour them over the onions and peas. Cook gently for about 10 minutes, pulling away the edges of the tortilla as it sets, to allow the uncooked egg to run underneath.

Meanwhile, preheat the broiler. When the tortilla is firm but still moist on top, brown the top under the broiler for about 5 minutes, until golden and set. Allow to cool for a few minutes.

Cover the skillet with a plate and carefully invert both skillet and plate. Remove the skillet. Place another plate on top of the tortilla and invert both plates and tortilla to turn it right-side up. Serve warm or at room temperature, cut into small wedges or bite-size pieces.

Ingredients
2 tbsp olive oil
2 onions, halved and sliced thinly
salt and ground black pepper
2 cups frozen peas, thawed
6 eggs
2 tsp chopped fresh mint

Serves 6

Pinchos
Skewered appetizers

*T*hese salty and piquant little skewers—the name means "thorn" or "spike" in Spanish—are served with drinks all over Spain. They're the perfect light bite to serve before a big meal.

Roll the anchovies into coils and thread each one onto a separate toothpick. Add a caper berry and cornichon to each stick and serve.

Ingredients
12 canned or marinated anchovy fillets, drained
12 caper berries
12 cornichons

Makes 12

Aceitunas aliñadas
Marinated green olives

Green olives marinated in herbs and garlic always seem to be at hand at any Spanish establishment. Served with toasted, salted almonds and often accompanying a frothy beer, these olives especially evoke the taste of Spain.

Lightly crush the olives with a mallet, or make slight slits in each olive with a knife, to ensure that the marinade permeates them. Place the olives in a sealable glass jar and add the remaining ingredients. Fill the jar with water and shake well. Marinate at room temperature for several days to a week.

Serve the olives with toasted almonds and fresh bread.

Ingredients
1 lb unpitted large green Spanish olives
7 cloves garlic, peeled and minced
2 bay leaves
½ medium lemon, sliced
1 tsp dried oregano
1 tsp ground fennel seeds
½ tsp dried thyme
½ tsp ground cumin
½ tsp dried rosemary
½ tsp Spanish paprika
½ tsp black pepper
toasted almonds
fresh bread

Makes 1 lb

Ensaladilla
Spanish potato salad

This traditional tapa is served throughout every region of Spain, with little variation. A poorly made version will taste like a mouthful of mayonnaise. On the other hand, a well-made ensaladilla is a perfectly balanced mixture of potatoes, hard-cooked eggs, and vegetables, using the mayonnaise solely to accent these other flavors. This colorful salad is served at nearly every tapas bar; it is even served free at times with an order of beer.

In a saucepan, cook the potatoes and carrot in lightly salted water. Bring to a boil and allow to simmer until almost tender. Fold in the peas and beans, and cook until all the vegetables are tender. Drain the vegetables and transfer them onto a serving platter. Add the onion, pepper, gherkins, capers, olives, and egg slices.

In a separate bowl, thoroughly combine the mayonnaise, lemon juice, and mustard. Add this mixture to the serving platter, mixing well to ensure all the ingredients are coated. Sprinkle with pepper and toss. Garnish with chopped parsley and refrigerate. Allow to stand at room temperature for about 1 hour immediately before serving to enhance the salad's flavor. As with any dish made with mayonnaise, ensaladilla should be refrigerated and will not keep for more than 1 to 2 days.

Ingredients
3 medium potatoes
1 large carrot, diced
5 tbsp shelled green peas
4 oz green beans
½ medium onion, chopped
1 small red bell pepper, chopped
4 cocktail gherkins, sliced
2 tbsp baby capers
12 anchovy-stuffed olives
1 hard-cooked egg, thinly sliced
5 fl. oz mayonnaise
1 tbsp lemon juice
1 tsp Dijon mustard
freshly ground black pepper, to taste
chopped fresh parsley, to garnish

Serves 4

Ensalada de cebolla y naranjas
Red onion and orange salad

Ingredients

4 ripe medium oranges, peeled

1 small red onion, finely sliced

2 tbsp raspberry vinegar

6 tbsp extra-virgin olive oil

salt and freshly ground pepper

4 tbsp golden raisins, covered for 20 mins in
   hot water, then drained

20 black olives, pitted

2 tbsp sunflower seeds

2 tbsp blanched almonds, finely chopped

sprigs of fresh mint, to garnish

Serves 4

*T*his popular and colorful salad lends a festive note to any tapas table, and is featured in many tapas bars throughout Spain. Some versions omit the red onion, or replace the raspberry vinegar with lemon juice. No matter which variation is served, however, this salad is tangy and refreshing on a hot summer day, and should always be served chilled.

Remove the white pith from the oranges and cut the fruit crosswise into ¼-inch (5-mm) slices. Arrange on a serving platter and scatter over the sliced red onion.

In a small bowl, whisk together the vinegar, olive oil, salt, and pepper. Spoon this dressing over the onion and oranges. Sprinkle with the raisins, olives, sunflower seeds, and almonds. Garnish with mint sprigs and serve chilled.

Ensalada de cabrales
Frisée and cabrales salad

*T*his salad is simple to prepare, and deeply refreshing when the weather is hot: frisée, with its refreshing, slightly bitter flavor; the peppers with their distinctive Mediterranean flavor; and the olives and blue cheese, with their pungent, salty bite.

Clean and core the frisée, and cut into bite-size pieces. Peel the peppers and cut into strips. Arrange the lettuce in a shallow bowl and garnish with the roasted bell peppers, blue cheese, and green olives. Dress with the olive oil and sherry vinegar. Serve immediately.

Ingredients
1 small head of frisée
2 red bell peppers, roasted
3 oz cabrales or other blue cheese
12 pimento-stuffed green olives
3 tbsp extra-virgin olive oil
1 tbsp sherry vinegar

Serves 4

Cabrales is aged in natural limestone caves, resulting in rich blue veins and a strong, acidic flavor.

Patatas bravas
Crisp spiced potatoes

Ingredients

3 tbsp olive oil, plus extra for frying

2 tbsp finely chopped onion

2 cloves garlic, finely chopped

1½ tbsp Spanish paprika

¼ tsp Tabasco sauce

¼ tsp dried thyme

4 fl. oz ketchup

4 fl. oz mayonnaise

salt and freshly ground black pepper

4 large potatoes, peeled and diced

chopped parsley, to garnish

Serves 4

Patatas bravas is a basic, traditional tapa as popular in elegant big-city establishments as it is in the more modest village hostelries. As with most tapas, each bar will have its own recipe, naturally believed to the best! Savor this mildly tangy version of patatas bravas with a chilled white wine.

In a saucepan, heat the 3 tablespoons olive oil over medium heat. Add the onion and garlic and sauté until the onion is soft. Turn off the heat, and add the paprika, Tabasco sauce, and thyme, stirring well. Transfer to a bowl and add the ketchup and mayonnaise. Season with salt and pepper to taste. Set aside.

Sprinkle the potatoes lightly with salt. In a large skillet, fry the potatoes in olive oil until cooked through and golden-brown, stirring occasionally. (Take care when adding the potatoes to the saucepan because the oil will splatter due to the salt.) Drain the potatoes on paper towels, check the seasoning, add more salt if necessary, and set aside.

Mix the potatoes with the sauce immediately before serving to ensure that the potatoes retain their crispness. Garnish with chopped parsley and serve warm.

Mejillones asados
Broiled mussels

*M*ussels are especially popular along the Bay of Biscay, but they *are enjoyed throughout Spain and are delicious cooked in this way. The crust of cheese and breadcrumbs protects the mussels from the fierce heat of the broiler, leaving them juicy and full of flavor.*

Check the mussels, discarding any that are open or ones that do not close when sharply tapped. Put the closed mussels in a large pan, add 3 tablespoons water, cover tightly, and cook over high heat for about 5 minutes, shaking the pan frequently, until the mussels have opened.

Discard any unopened shells. Snap off and discard the top shell of each mussel and arrange the shells with mussels in a flameproof dish.

Preheat the broiler. Combine the breadcrumbs, Parmesan cheese, garlic, parsley, and oil, and season with black pepper. Spoon the crumb mixture onto the mussels, then broil them for about 2 minutes until golden and bubbling. Serve immediately.

Ingredients
1 lb 2 oz mussels, cleaned
4 tbsp dry breadcrumbs
3 tbsp freshly grated Parmesan cheese
2 garlic cloves, crushed
2 tbsp chopped fresh parsley
2½ tbsp olive oil
freshly ground black pepper

Serves 4

Gambas en gabardinas
Battered shrimp

Ingredients
½ cup flour
pinch of salt
3 tbsp oil or melted butter
6 fl. oz tepid water
pinch of cayenne pepper
1 lb large shrimp in the shell
olive oil for deep frying
1 large egg white
1 lemon, cut into wedges

Serves 4

*T*he light, crisp batter keeps these tender shrimp moist in the hot oil.

To make the batter, put the flour and salt in a blender or bowl, work in the oil or butter, and add the warm water. Stir to make a smooth batter. Add a pinch of cayenne pepper. Leave this to stand, and peel the shrimp.

Heat the deep-frying oil to top heat in an electric fryer. Whisk the egg white until it forms soft peaks, and fold this into the batter.

Dip each shrimp into the batter and drop into the oil. Let the shrimp puff up and color for about 30 seconds, then remove with a slotted spoon onto paper towel. Serve at once with the lemon wedges.

Ensalada de mariscos
Seafood salad

*Y*ou could use any combination of seafood for this salad, but the mixture of scallops, shrimp, calamari, and mussels is particularly rich in flavors and textures.

Fill a large stockpot three-quarters of the way full with water and bring to a boil. Add the lemons, bay leaves, hot sauce, and salt. Cook for a few minutes, then add the shrimp and cook for about 4 minutes.

Remove the shrimp, leaving the cooking water in the pot, and immediately transfer the shrimp to a bowl of ice water. Bring the cooking water back to a boil and repeat the process with the scallops, cooking for 3 minutes, and then the calamari, cooking for 1 minute. Add more ice to the water as necessary.

Coat the bottom of a skillet with olive oil and cook the garlic until it is golden. Add the clams and wine, adding more wine if needed. Cover and steam for 4 minutes, or until the first clams begin to open. Add the mussels, and cook until both the clams and mussels open.

Remove the clams and mussels from the pan and set aside, leaving the pan on the heat. Add the thyme to the pan and reduce the broth by three-quarters. Strain and let cool until about room temperature.

Combine the onion, celery, roasted pepper, basil, 1 tablespoon olive oil, and lime juice in a bowl. Cut the shrimp and scallops in half and add to the bowl, along with the strained broth. Remove the mussels and clams from the shells and add to the mix. Check for seasoning, adding salt and pepper as needed. Let marinate in the refrigerator for at least 30 minutes before serving, garnished with basil leaves.

Ingredients

2 lemons, cut in half
2 bay leaves
½ tsp hot red pepper sauce
Salt, to season
8 oz shrimp, peeled, cleaned, and deveined
ice water
4 oz scallops
3 medium calamari (squid),
    cut into rings
olive oil, for frying, plus 1 tbsp for marinade
2 cloves garlic, sliced
24 Little Neck clams, cleaned
2 fl. oz white wine, or more if needed
24 mussels, cleaned
¼ bunch thyme, stems removed and finely
    chopped
1 small red onion, finely chopped
1 stalk of celery, finely chopped
1 roasted red bell pepper, finely chopped
4 fresh basil leaves, finely chopped
½ tsp fresh lime juice
basil leaves, to garnish

Serves 4

Calamares rellenos
Stuffed squid

Ingredients

12 oz ground veal
12 oz ground pork
1 tsp dried oregano
1 tsp ground cumin
3½ fl. oz cup olive oil
3 whole garlic cloves, peeled
2 medium white onions, finely chopped
1 small green bell pepper,
    finely chopped
8 fl. oz dry white wine
8 fl. oz tomato sauce
8 green olives, pitted and sliced
¼ cup raisins
salt and freshly ground black pepper,
12 extra-large calamari (squid) tubes, cleaned
toothpicks
1 red bell pepper, finely chopped
2 garlic cloves, finely chopped
10-oz can whole tomatoes, crushed by hand
1 bay leaf
salad, to serve
fresh parsley, to garnish

Serves 4

Stuffing and stewing squid is an excellent way to deal with large, slightly tough squid. Instead of tomato sauce, you could serve the squid sprinkled with cheese or accompanied by a dip such as garlic-flavored mayonnaise.

Thoroughly combine the veal, pork, oregano, and cumin in a mixing bowl.

Heat ¼ cup of the olive oil in a skillet and, over a medium heat, cook the 3 whole garlic cloves, 1 of the onions, and the green bell pepper until soft, for about 4 minutes.

Add the meat mixture, half of the wine, and the tomato sauce. Cover and cook over a medium to low heat for about 15 minutes.

Uncover the pan, mix in the olives and raisins, and cook for a further 15 minutes, or until the liquid is almost fully reduced, making sure that the meat is still moist. Season with salt and pepper. Remove from the heat and let cool.

Stuff the calamari with the meat mixture and close the ends with toothpicks. Set aside. Preheat the oven to 325°F (190°C).

Heat the remaining olive oil in a medium saucepan over a medium heat and cook the remaining onion, red bell pepper, and garlic until soft, for about 4 minutes.

Add the tomatoes and the bay leaf, and bring the mixture to a boil. Immediately remove from the heat and pour into a 9-inch rectangular baking pan.

Arrange the stuffed calamari in the pan and cover with aluminum foil. Bake in the oven for 45 minutes or until the calamari are tender. Serve with a side salad and garnish with parsley.

Escabeche de bonito
Pickled tuna

*E*scabeche is a method of preparing fish in a vinegar- or citrus-based marinade. Sometimes escabeche of chicken, rabbit, or pork are served instead of fish. Spain borrowed the technique from the Moors, and it has since been transplanted to Latin America, becoming especially popular in Peru, Mexico, and Puerto Rico.

Combine the vinegar, olive oil, onions, bell pepper, capers, paprika, and olives in a mixing bowl. Set aside.

Heat the 2 tablespoons olive oil in a medium sauté pan, and cook the tuna and garlic for 2 minutes on each side. Set aside.

Add the marinade and cook for 4 minutes. Remove from the heat and season with salt and pepper. Place in the refrigerator and marinate overnight before serving, garnished with lemon wedges.

Ingredients

4 tbsp white wine vinegar
6 fl. oz extra virgin olive oil
2 medium white onions, finely sliced
1 medium green bell pepper, finely sliced
¼ cup capers
½ tsp paprika
10 large green olives, pitted and sliced
2 tbsp olive oil
3 lb fresh tuna, cleaned, deboned, and cut into 1-inch slices
2 garlic cloves, finely sliced
salt and freshly ground black pepper
lemon wedges

Serves 4

Ceviche de gambas
Shrimp salad

Ingredients

2 lb shrimp or 1 lb shrimp
 and 1 lb white fish

2 pints water

20 fl. oz lime juice

2 medium red onions,
 finely chopped

2 tbsp soy sauce

salt and freshly ground
 black pepper

2 cucumbers, cubed

1 red bell pepper, seeded and
 cubed

1 bunch fresh dill, chopped

Tabasco sauce, to taste

lime wedges, to serve

Serves 8

*T*his salad is bursting with fresh flavors, combining sweet shrimp with a herby, salty–sour dressing. The shrimp are not cooked—though they look and taste it—so you must buy the very freshest.

Shell and devein the shrimp, and skin and clean fish if using. Place in a large bowl.

Mix the ingredients for the marinade together (water, lime juice, red onions, soy sauce, salt, and pepper) and pour over the shrimp. Marinate for 20 minutes.

Add the cucumber, pepper cubes, and dill. Toss together in the bowl.

Spoon onto plates or into small bowls. Sprinkle with pepper and Tabasco sauce. Serve with lime wedges.

Camarones al ajillo
Garlic shrimp

*T*his recipe is packed with garlic, so you may wish to reduce the quantities. It is based on a Spanish peasant dish made with plump, fresh shrimp, and is simple but extremely tasty. Serve with plenty of bread to mop up the juices.

Remove the heads from the shrimp, but do not peel. Wash and pat dry the shrimp and place in a shallow glass dish. Add the lime juice and oregano. Cover and chill for 2 hours.

When ready to cook, heat 2 tablespoons of the olive oil in a skillet and gently fry the garlic for 1 minute, stirring, making sure it does not over brown.

Raise the heat and add the shrimp with the marinating juices and the remaining olive oil. Stir-fry for 5 minutes until the shrimp are pink all over, then season with the salt and black pepper.

Pile the shrimp onto warmed plates, sprinkle with the parsley, and serve with the wedges of lime and some crusty bread.

Ingredients
2 lb raw extra-large shrimp
juice of 2 limes
½ tsp dried oregano
6 tbsp extra-virgin Spanish olive oil
8 cloves garlic, finely chopped
salt and freshly ground black pepper
2 tbsp chopped fresh parsley
lime wedges, to garnish

Serves 4

Merluza española
Spanish-style haddock

Ingredients

1 lb haddock fillet or similar white fish, skinned

3 tbsp fruity olive oil

1 small onion, finely sliced

2 cloves garlic, finely sliced

4 oz sliced mushrooms

1 small red bell pepper, seeded and sliced

1 small green bell pepper, seeded and sliced

salt and freshly ground black pepper

4 fl. oz white wine vinegar

3 fl. oz water

1 tbsp sugar

Serves 4

*S*erve with crusty bread for a summer lunch or light supper.

Cut the fish into bite-size pieces. Heat two tablespoons of the oil in a skillet and fry the fish until just cooked. Transfer it to a glass dish. Heat the remaining oil in the skillet; add the onion and garlic and cook until soft but not browned. Stir in the mushrooms and peppers and cook for a further 1–2 minutes—the vegetables should retain a crisp texture. Spoon the vegetables over the fish and season lightly.

Pour the vinegar and water into the skillet and bring to a boil. Stir in the sugar until dissolved, then pour the liquid over the fish and vegetables. Leave to cool, then cover and place in the refrigerator for 24 hours.

The Plaza de la Esperanza fish market in Santander, Cantabria.

Cangrejos de rio con tomate
Freshwater crawfish in tomato sauce

Crawfish served with a simple fresh tomato sauce make a delicious treat of an appetizer. You could use other shellfish, such as crab or lobster, if you prefer.

Heat about 3 tablespoons of the olive oil in a large, deep skillet. Fry the onions and garlic in the oil until the onion is soft and translucent. While the onions and garlic are cooking, chop the tomatoes finely. Add the wine and the rest of the oil to the skillet, along with the tomatoes and their juice. Sprinkle in a pinch of cayenne pepper. Simmer for about 10 minutes, stirring often, until the sauce has thickened slightly. Season to taste. Keep warm while you cook the crawfish.

Bring plenty of water to a boil in a large stockpot. Add the live crawfish to the boiling water and cook until they turn red. Remove the pan from the heat and drain.

Add the crawfish to the skillet with the tomato sauce and stir well, coating the crawfish thoroughly with the sauce.

Ingredients
4 tbsp olive oil
1 onion, finely chopped
3 large cloves garlic, finely chopped
4 large tomatoes
pinch cayenne pepper
2 lb live crawfish
6 fl. oz white wine
salt and freshly ground pepper

Serves 2 as a main course,
   4 as an appetizer

Croquetas de jamón
Ham croquettes

Ingredients
olive oil for frying
3 lb smoked ham, chopped
1 onion, chopped
2 red bell peppers, chopped
2 garlic cloves, sliced
2 tbsp tomato paste
4 tbsp fresh chopped parsley
½ tsp freshly grated nutmeg
4 fl. oz heavy cream
4 oz all-purpose flour
salt and freshly ground black pepper
2 eggs, lightly beaten
2 cups cracker meal
vegetable oil for frying

Makes 6–8

Croquettes, originally from France, long ago became a delicacy and favorite snack throughout the Spanish-speaking world. This is a typical Iberian recipe. You could replace the smoked ham with cooked, shredded chicken.

Heat the olive oil in a large skillet and cook the ham, onion, bell peppers, and garlic for about 8 minutes. Stir in the tomato paste and cook until it caramelizes. Add the parsley, nutmeg, and heavy cream. Sprinkle in 2 ounces of the flour and season with salt and pepper. Let the mixture cool for a while until about room temperature.

Put the mixture through a meat grinder, or grind in a food processor. Shape the mixture into finger-shaped sticks, or small patties.

Bread these croquetas by first dipping them into the remaining flour, then the eggs, and finally into the cracker meal.

Pour 1 inch of vegetable oil into a skillet and heat to medium—375°F (190°C) on a frying thermometer, or until a cube of bread dropped in turns golden brown in 60 seconds. Fry the croquetas until golden brown.

Arroz amarillo
Spanish rice

Rice has been grown in Valencia since it was brought to Iberia by the Moors in the tenth century. The supreme Spanish crops are calasparra and bomba, both short-grained rices which retain their shape in cooking without gaining creamy soft edges—making them ideal for paella and other dishes. Any white rice can be used to good effect in this simple, traditional Spanish preparation.

Heat the olive oil in a medium saucepan over a medium heat. Add the onion and cook until soft. Add the rice, stirring, until coated with the oil.

Add the water and bring to a boil. Season generously with salt and add the bay leaves and turmeric. Cook over a medium heat, uncovered, for about 20 minutes, until most of the water has been absorbed by the rice.

Ingredients
4 tbsp olive oil
1 large onion, peeled and diced
1¾ lb white rice
2½ pints water
salt
2 bay leaves
¼ tsp turmeric

Serves 4

Churros
Spanish doughnuts

Ingredients
7 oz self-rising flour
2 tbsp sugar
¼ tsp salt
4 tbsp olive oil
6 fl. oz water
1 egg, beaten
oil for deep frying
superfine sugar for dusting

Serves 4

*C*hurros are long thin strips of fluted dough fried to form loops. If thicker and straight, they are called porras, and if in the shape of a ring or hollow ball, buñuelos.

Pass the flour, sugar, and salt through a sifter onto a plate. Set aside. In a saucepan, bring the oil and water to a boil. Remove from the heat and quickly add the flour mixture. Beat vigorously until smooth. Gradually beat in the egg until the mixture forms a smooth, thick paste.

Half-fill a large, deep skillet suitable for deep-frying with oil and heat to 375°F (190°C), or until a cube of bread dropped in turns golden brown in 60 seconds. Spoon the dough into a pastry bag fitted with a ½-inch (1-cm) nozzle, and pipe 3 or 4 pieces of dough into the hot oil, using the nozzle to form the dough into spirals or horseshoe shapes. Fry for 2–3 minutes or until golden. Using a slotted spoon, transfer the dough pieces to paper towels and drain.

Fry the remaining mixture in the same way. Generously dust all the fried pastries with sugar and serve hot with coffee or hot chocolate.

Arroz con leche
Rice pudding

*T*his simple milk-based pudding has become popular across the Spanish-speaking world. A delicious variation from Argentina and Uruguay is to serve it with a spoonful of dulce de leche.

Cook the rice, water, salt, lemon rind, and cinnamon sticks in a medium saucepan over a medium heat for about 15 minutes.

Once the rice begins to split open, add the evaporated milk and sugar. Cook over a very low heat, stirring continuously, until the mixture becomes creamy. Remove and reserve the cinnamon sticks.

Remove from the heat and add the vanilla. Chill in individual serving cups and serve garnished with ground cinnamon and the reserved cinnamon sticks.

Ingredients
3½ oz white long-grain rice, rinsed
¾ pints water
½ tsp salt
rind of 1 lemon, grated
3 cinnamon sticks
10-oz can evaporated milk
7 oz superfine sugar
1 tsp vanilla extract
ground cinnamon, to garnish

Serves 4

Dulce de cascaras
Candied citrus rind

Ingredients
3 large ripe grapefruit
water
salt
14 oz superfine sugar
1¾ pints water
cream cheese

Serves 6–8

*C*andying your own rind makes you realize how poorly store-bought rind often imitates the real thing. This is a delicious dessert, especially if the acid flavor is softened by serving it with something creamy and slightly sweet, such as cream cheese.

Quarter and peel the grapefruits, being sure to remove as much of the bitter white pith as possible. Cover the shells in cold, salted water for 24 hours, changing the water regularly to remove bitterness.

The following day, drain the shells and discard the soaking water. Place the shells into a large saucepan with fresh, cold water to cover and bring to a boil over a medium to high heat. Discard the water as soon as it reaches a boil and repeat the procedure.

Drain the shells and pat them dry with paper towels to remove all the moisture. Place them in a large saucepan with the sugar and water and cook over a low heat, uncovered, until the shells are soft and transparent and the syrup has thickened, for about 1½–2 hours.

Let the shells and syrup cool to room temperature. Transfer to a bowl and refrigerate, covered, until ready to serve. Serve chilled with cream cheese.

Natillas de chocolate
Chocolate pudding

*N*atillas *is a generic name for a type of Spanish custard dish.*
This chocolate version is creamy, sweet, and comforting.

Place the milk, cinnamon, and salt in a saucepan and bring to a boil. Remove from the heat and set aside.

Beat the egg yolks and sugar in a mixing bowl. In a separate bowl, thoroughly dissolve the flour in the water and add to the yolk mixture. Add the boiled milk and then strain into a saucepan. Place the mixture over a medium heat and add the chocolate, stirring constantly, until the chocolate melts and the mixture becomes thick. Stir in the vanilla.

Pour into bowls, let cool to room temperature, and chill until ready to serve. Serve with a little whipped cream and decorate with slivered cinnamon sticks.

Ingredients
4 pints milk
1 cinnamon stick
¼ teaspoon salt
8 medium egg yolks
10 oz sugar
4 tbsp all-purpose flour
2 fl. oz water
8 oz semi-sweet chocolate
1 tsp vanilla extract
whipped cream, to serve
cinnamon sticks, to garnish

Serves 10

Compota de peras
Pear compote

Ingredients

2 lb pears
juice ½ lemon
½ lb superfine sugar
¾ pint water
1 cinnamon stick

Serves 4

*P*ears usually thrive in cool temperate locations, and they seem to have originated in the foothills of a mountain range in western China. But they are widely cultivated in Spain and are popular in simple desserts such as this one.

Peel and core the pears and cut each one into about six pieces. Place in a saucepan and quickly sprinkle lemon juice over them to prevent discoloration. Add the sugar, water, and cinnamon stick to the pan and bring to a boil. Simmer for 10–15 minutes, until the pears are very soft but still hold their shape. Serve warm or at room temperature, heaped into glasses with some of the cooking syrup.

Sangría tradicional
Basic sangría

A very simple, unfussy sangría. While this sangría is delicious as it is, this recipe intentionally leaves ample room for improvisation and additions, and should therefore be used as a springboard to create your own unique sangría recipes. The unaltered recipe below, however, would meet with the approval of strict sangría traditionalists.

Combine all ingredients except for the club soda in a large punch bowl or serving pitcher, mixing well. Refrigerate overnight. Immediately before serving, mix in the club soda for added fizz. Ladle into cups with ice cubes.

Ingredients

26 fl. oz dry red wine

1 tbsp sugar

juice of 1 large orange

juice of 1 large lemon

1 large orange, sliced thin crosswise

1 large lemon, sliced thin crosswise

2 medium peaches, peeled, pitted, and cut into chunks

8 fl. oz sparkling water

Makes 4 glasses

Sangría blanca
White sangría

*B*ursting with sparkling flavor, this clear version of sangría is unique in its use of ice cubes made from apple juice. For parties, this can be served in a large, transparent punch bowl next to a transparent bowl containing traditional red sangría. This pairing provides a beautiful contrast, provided they are not immediately consumed by eager guests, as is often the case.

To make the apple-juice ice cubes, pour the apple juice into two ice trays and freeze until the sangría is ready to serve.

Combine the water, mint leaves, sugar, and cinnamon in a small saucepan, and bring to a boil over medium heat. Reduce the heat and simmer for several minutes. Remove from the heat and allow to cool. Once the mixture has cooled to room temperature, remove and discard the mint and cinnamon sticks. Transfer the remaining mixture to a large serving bowl.

Add the wine, peaches, pears, and the orange and lemon slices to the serving bowl. Mix well, cover, and refrigerate overnight. Immediately before serving, mix in the sparkling apple cider and the apple-juice ice cubes. Garnish with fresh mint leaves, if desired.

Ingredients

apple juice, for ice cubes
10 fl. oz water
1 small bunch fresh mint
3½ oz sugar
3 cinnamon sticks
26 fl. oz dry white wine
2 medium peaches, peeled, pitted, and sliced
2 small pears, cut into chunks
2 medium oranges, sliced crosswise
2 small lemons, sliced crosswise
24 fl. oz sparkling apple cider
mint leaves, to garnish (optional)

Makes 8 glasses

CHAPTER 2

Northern Spain

Galicia, in the north-western tip of the Iberian peninsula, feels very remote from the rest of Spain. It has preserved its dense forests and beautiful fjord-like estuaries, called rías, and is often windswept and rainy. Unsurprisingly, fish dominates the cuisine of this coastal region. Farther east, Asturias is the center of Spain's mining country. It is famed for its excellent apples and milk, as well as the bean dish called fabada. Cantabria is the mountainous corridor between the Basque Country and the rest of Spain, with its culture centered on the casino city of Santander and a cuisine based around nourishing dishes of game, beans, and fish.

Fishing boats in a Galician harbor. Sea-fishing remains a major industry along Spain's northern coast. The region of Galicia is sometimes referred to as the "costa do morisco"—seafood coast—by its inhabitants.

Caldo gallego
Galician bean, pork, and greens soup

Traditionally this is a spring soup, made with the tender leaves of young spring turnips and a special variety of new potatoes, called cachelos. The flavor is enriched by the use of salt meat. Use spare ribs or salt pork belly, whichever is most readily available.

If using pork ribs, rub them well with salt. Alternatively, salt pork must be blanched. Put it with the ham hock (gammon knuckle) in a pan, cover with cold water, and bring to a boil. Simmer for 5 minutes, then drain. Cube the pork.

Drain the beans and put them, with the meat and bones, into an ovenproof dish. Add 3¼ pints water, bring to a simmer, and skim off any scum. Cook gently, covered, for an hour.

Add the potatoes and simmer until done. Remove all bones from the pot and taste the stock. Season with salt and pepper as necessary. Add the greens and simmer for 5–10 minutes. Return all meat from the bones to the pan. To thicken the liquid a little, mash in a few of the potatoes.

Ingredients
9 oz dried haricot beans, soaked overnight
¾ lb pork belly ribs or 4 oz salt pork
salt and freshly ground black pepper
1 lb smoked ham hock (gammon knuckle)
1 lb new potatoes
7 oz tender turnip leaves or kale

Serves 6

The cathedral of Santiago de Compostela—the capital of Galicia. It is here that the Feast of Saint James, one of the biggest Spanish fiestas in the Christian calendar, takes place annually.

Sopa de castañas
Creamy chestnut soup

Ingredients
1 lb chestnuts
salt and freshly ground black pepper
1 thick slice bread
4 tbsp olive oil
2 tbsp red wine vinegar
1¼ pints light stock
⅛ tsp cinnamon

Serves 4

*I*n Galicia, chestnuts are often used where beans or potatoes might be used in the rest of Europe. They are softened by the paprika juices of fried sausages, or heaped round roast pork or duck. Here they make a creamy winter soup, lightly spiced with a hint of cinnamom.

Slash the chestnut shells across the fat part of the nut. Drop into a pan and cover with salted cold water. Bring to a boil and cook for 30 minutes. Let cool without removing from the water. Peel the chestnuts and remove the brown skins. Chop them coarsely.

Fry the bread in the oil, then put it in a blender or food processor and purée with the vinegar. Reserve a handful of the chopped chestnuts to add texture to the soup. Add the rest to the blender, a little at a time, with some of the stock. Purée to a cream. Flavor discreetly with cinnamon. Add the reserved chopped chestnuts, heat through, and serve.

Empanadas
Galician stuffed pastries

*E*mpanadas are most often associated with Latin America—but in fact, these crisp and tasty turnovers originated in Galicia.

Preheat the oven to 350°F (175°C). Heat the oil in a large skillet. When the oil is hot, add the chopped onions and sauté for 3 minutes, until the onions are translucent. Add both paprikas, red pepper flakes, cumin, and vinegar and stir until well combined. Add the ground beef and cook until the meat is browned. Drain half the fat from the skillet. On a lightly floured surface, roll out the puff pastry ¼ inch thick. Using a 5-inch cutter, cut out circles of pastry. One package of puff pastry should yield 8 rounds.

Using a pastry brush, glaze the top edge of each circle with water. Spoon 2 tablespoons filling onto the lower half of the circle. Sprinkle each with raisins and olives. Fold the top half of the circle over, pressing the edges to seal. Crimp the edge by twisting the pastry inward, from one side to the other. This will prevent the juices from leaking during baking. Glaze the tops of the empanadas with the egg. Prick the crust with a fork near the seam to allow steam to escape. Place the empanadas on a baking sheet lined with parchment paper, and bake for 25 minutes, or until the filling is hot and the crust is golden.

Ingredients
2 tbsp olive oil
2 medium onions, chopped
2 tsp smoked sweet paprika
½ tsp hot paprika
½ tsp crushed red pepper flakes
1 tsp ground cumin
1 tbsp white vinegar
1 lb lean ground beef
16 oz puff pastry, defrosted if frozen
¼ cup raisins
½ cup pitted green olives, chopped
1 large egg, lightly beaten

Makes 8

Empanadillas de atún y de queso
Tuna and goat cheese empanadillas

*E*mpanadillas, the smaller, pocket-size versions of empanadas, are generally served as tapas. Because they can be eaten with the hands, they are the perfect food for parties or snacks.

Heat the olive oil in a skillet over medium heat. Add the onion and garlic and sauté for about 5 minutes or until softened. Remove from the heat and set aside. Using a fork, mash the tuna with the onion, garlic, goat cheese, olives, pine nuts, capers, paprika, salt, and pepper. Set aside.

On a floured surface, roll out the pastry to ⅛-inch (3-mm) thickness. Using a 3-inch cookie cutter, cut out as many dough circles as the dough will allow, rerolling the dough sheets if necessary. Cupping each dough round in your hand, spoon about 1 teaspoon of the filling into the center of it, then brush the edges with a little water. Fold the dough over the mixture to form a crescent. Pinch the edges of crescent to seal the dough closed. Use the back of a fork to further press the edges of the dough together.

Transfer to a greased baking sheet, and repeat the process with the remaining dough rounds and pastry. Bake in the oven at 400° F (200°C) for 20–25 minutes or until golden. Allow to cool for 5 minutes before serving.

Ingredients
1 tbsp olive oil
5 tbsp minced onion
2 cloves garlic, minced
6 oz canned tuna, packed in olive oil
4 oz goat cheese
3 oz pimento-stuffed olives, chopped
5 tbsp toasted pine nuts
5 tbsp capers, chopped
1 tsp paprika
salt and pepper, to taste
16 oz puff pastry, defrosted if frozen

Serves 6–8

Paella de salchicha y venera
Galician sausage and scallop paella

*G*alicia is famous throughout Spain for the extraordinary quality of its seafood. Due to its exposed position on the north–western tip of Spain, Galicia has an inordinately large number of fish available to it. In fact, Galician fishermen bring in more scallops each year than anywhere else in Spain. With a nod toward Galicia, this paella teams scallops with shrimp and sausage to lend the rice a rich, tender flavor. Enjoy this dish with a chilled glass of Galician wine, such as Albariño.

Heat the olive oil in a paella pan over medium heat. Add the onion and cook for 5 minutes. Throw in the bell pepper and cook for a further 5 minutes. Add the garlic and continue to cook for about a further 3 minutes. Add the sausage and cook for about 8 minutes, or until done.

Mix in the rice and sauté for about a further 5 minutes. Pour in the broth and saffron and cook for a further 15 minutes. Add the wine, scallops, shrimp, peas, tomatoes, salt, and pepper. Continue cooking for 8 minutes or until the liquid has been absorbed and the rice is tender. Taste for seasoning, and serve at once.

Ingredients
2 fl. oz olive oil
1 medium yellow onion, chopped
1 large red bell pepper, chopped
2 cloves garlic, minced
8 oz Kielbasa sausage, skinned and chopped
1 lb 6 oz rice
2¼ pints fish broth
½ tsp saffron
4 fl. oz dry white wine
8 oz scallops
12 oz uncooked shrimp, peeled and deveined
10 oz frozen peas, defrosted
3 medium tomatoes, peeled, seeded, and
  chopped
salt and white pepper, to taste

Serves 6–8

Pulpo a la gallega
Galician-style octopus

Ingredients

1 gallon water, salted

1 lemon, cut in half

1 medium white onion, peeled
  and cut in half

2 bay leaves

1 bunch fresh parsley, stems left whole and
  leaves chopped

2 tbsp hot red pepper sauce

one 6- to 8-lb octopus

2 medium baking potatoes, washed

¼ cup olive oil

3 cloves garlic, peeled and sliced

½ medium white onion, finely sliced

3 tsp paprika

Salt and fresh ground black pepper, to season

Serves 4

*T*his tender stewed octopus dish is the signature meal of Galicia. If octopus are not easily available, you could substitute squid. But be sure to use large squid: the tender baby ones are not suited to this long, slow cooking.

Hold the octopus by the tentacles and bang it against the countertop several times to tenderize it. Combine the water, lemon halves, onion halves, bay leaves, whole parsley stems, hot sauce, and octopus in a large stockpot and bring to a boil over a high heat. Cook for about 1½ hours or until the octopus is tender. During the last 30 minutes, add the potatoes.

Remove the potatoes and set aside to let cool to room temperature. Remove the octopus and let cool for a few minutes.

Peel the octopus, which must be done while it is still hot, and completely remove all the ink and the suction cups. Do not rinse the octopus during this process. Keep a bowl of ice water nearby to use to cool your hands. Cut the peeled octopus into 1½-inch pieces and set aside.

Peel the potatoes and cut into 2-inch cubes. Heat the olive oil in a medium sauté pan and cook the garlic over a medium heat. Add the onion, potatoes, and octopus. Add the paprika and chopped parsley. Mix well and season with salt and pepper.

Vieiras de Santiago
Saint James's baked scallops

*E*very restaurant in the old town of Santiago offers this dish on *Saint James's Day, for scallops have always been associated with this saint and scallop shells are still the badge of the many pilgrims who visit his shrine. Galician scallops are huge, and benefit from the robust flavors of brandy and tomato which make up this sauce.*

Heat the butter and 1 tablespoon of oil and quickly fry the scallops for 2 minutes on each side. Shelled or defrosted scallops make a lot of liquid, so remove them when cooked, then boil this off.

Warm the brandy in a ladle, flame it, and pour over the scallops. Then spoon them into upper scallop shells or small heatproof dishes.

Add another 2 tablespoons of oil to the pan and fry the onion gently, adding the garlic as it softens. Add the chopped tomatoes, paprika, and cayenne pepper, and cook until the tomato has reduced to a sauce. Moisten with the wine, add salt and pepper to taste, and spoon over the scallops.

Mix the breadcrumbs and parsley and sprinkle thinly on top of the scallops. Heat through for 2–3 minutes under a low broiler and serve immediately.

Ingredients

1 tbsp butter
3 tbsp olive oil
14 oz shelled scallops
4 tbsp brandy
1 onion, finely chopped
3 garlic cloves, finely chopped
7 oz ripe tomatoes, skinned and deseeded
1 tsp paprika
pinch of cayenne pepper
4 fl. oz dry white wine
salt and freshly ground black peppper
3 tbsp fine breadcrumbs
1 tbsp chopped fresh parsley

Serves 4

Fabada asturiana
Bean and sausage pot

Ingredients

1 lb 10 oz dried white beans

1½ lb salt pork belly (or salt brisket)

1½ lb ham hocks

6 black peppercorns, crushed

1 tsp paprika

pinch of powdered saffron

1 bay leaf

2 tbsp oil (optional)

4 garlic cloves, chopped

1 lb chorizo or other smoked sausage

6 oz morcilla or other blood sausage

Serves 6

*I*n Asturias, this beanpot is flavored with local specialties such as lacon, the cured front leg of a pig. Salt pork and cured beef make good substitutes. Cured sausages are also added, giving an incredible richness to the flat, white beans.

Choose a stockpot that holds at least 10 pints. Cover the beans, in a bowl, with plenty of boiling water. Put the salt meat into the pot and cover with cold water. Bring to a boil, then drain the meat and return to the stockpot. Drain the beans and add them to the pot with the peppercorns, paprika, saffron, and bay leaf. Add 4 pints water. Bring slowly to a boil, then simmer very gently, over minimum heat, for 2 hours. Check occasionally that the beans are still covered, but do not stir, or they will break up.

Remove the meat and let cool a little. Strip off the skin and fat and take about 2 tablespoons of chopped fat for frying (or use oil). Sweat the fat in a skillet. In the fat it makes, fry the garlic lightly, then spoon it into the beans.

Slice the chorizo and morcilla and fry them until cooked through. Stir into the pot with the fat they leach into the pan. Remove all the meat from the ham hock. Chop it, and the salt pork or beef, and return to the pot. Simmer for a few minutes. Check the seasonings and serve.

Habitas refritas
Refried kidney beans

*T*he translation of this recipe as "refried" can cause confusion, as it is often interpreted as "fried again." In fact, the Spanish term *refrito* is actually a reference to overfrying the mashed beans so that they dry out enough to retain a shape in which they can be served.

Place the first 7 ingredients in a pan, bring to a boil, and simmer for 40 minutes.

Place one-quarter of the total in a food processor and purée. Remix the puréed beans with the whole beans.

Chop the bacon and place in boiling water for 10 minutes to remove the saltiness. Remove from the water and drain.

Heat the butter in a skillet and fry the bacon. Add the beans, little by little, and mash with the back of a spoon. Season well.

The beans should go into a thick purée. Season, sprinkle with parsley, and serve. The more often you refry the beans, the better they taste.

Ingredients
1-lb can kidney beans
1 red chile, seeded and chopped
1 medium onion, finely chopped
2 tsp garlic, crushed
1 tsp paprika
salt and freshly ground
   black pepper
2 pints water
6 slices good bacon, without the rind
2¼ oz butter
parsley, to serve

Serves 2–4

Leche frita
Crisp custard squares

Ingredients

18 fl. oz creamy milk

3 strips lemon zest

½ cinnamon stick

4 oz superfine sugar, plus extra for dusting

4 tbsp cornstarch

2 tbsp flour

3 large egg yolks

sunflower oil for frying

2 eggs, to coat

6 tbsp breadcrumbs

ground cinnamon

Serves 6

*T*his recipe, popular throughout northern Spain, combines a meltingly creamy center with a crunchy coating. The squares can be enjoyed hot or cold.

Bring the milk, lemon zest, cinnamon stick, and sugar to a boil in a saucepan, stirring gently. Cover and leave off the heat to infuse for 20 minutes.

Put the cornstarch and flour in a bowl and beat in the egg yolks with a wooden spoon. Start adding some of the milk until the batter is smooth. Strain in the rest of the hot milk, then pour back into the pan. Cook over a low heat, stirring continuously. It will not curdle, but does thicken unevenly if you let it. Cook for a couple of minutes until it becomes a thick custard that separates from the side of the pan. Beat it hard with the spoon to keep it smooth. Pour into a small baking tray, smoothing to a square about 8 x 8 inches and ½ inch deep. Cool and then chill.

Pour oil into a shallow skillet to a depth of about ½ inch and heat until very hot. Cut the custard into 12 squares. Beat the eggs on a plate and lift half the squares into the egg with a metal spatula. Coat and then lift them onto a tray of crumbs (big stale crumbs are best, but dried will do) and coat all round.

Lift them with a clean palette knife into the oil and fry for a couple of minutes, spooning the oil over the top, until golden. Reserve on paper towel while you fry the second batch. Dust with sugar and cinnamon before serving. They can be served hot, but are excellent when chilled.

Carajitos
Hazelnut macaroons

*N*ut bushes are a key part of the northern Spanish landscape, so it is not surprising that excellent nuts are used to make the best biscuits. Children eat these hazelnut macaroons with a glass of milk at the end of the afternoon.

Toast the nuts in the oven while it heats to 375°F (190°C). Grind them in a food processor. Do not over-grind or they will become very oily.

Rub some sugar over the grater to pick up leftover lemon oil, then rub the zest thoroughly into all the sugar. Sprinkle with cinnamon.

Whisk the egg whites until they form soft peaks. Stir about a quarter of the egg white into the ground nuts to soften them. Sprinkle about half the sugar over the whites and gently fold in, then fold in the remainder alternately with the nut mixture.

Dot walnut-size pieces onto greased foil on 1 or 2 baking sheets, pressing them out gently and spacing them an inch apart. Bake for 15 minutes until golden brown. Let cool for 5 minutes, then remove from the foil.

Ingredients
5 oz blanched hazelnuts
5 oz superfine sugar
finely grated zest ½ lemon
pinch ground cinnamon
2 large egg whites
butter for greasing

Makes about 20

CHAPTER 3

The Pyrenees

The map shows cities including BILBAO, PAMPLONA, LOGRONO, and ZARAGOZA, and regions labeled Basque Country, Navarre, La Rioja, and Aragon.

The Pyrenees divide the Iberian peninsula from the rest of Europe. There are few passes across the mountains, and those which are to be found are at high altitudes. Geography has conspired to isolate some communities sheltered by the mountains, protecting local cultures such as—most famously—the Basque people. The other Pyrenean regions in Spain's north-east (Catalonia, Aragon, La Rioja, and Navarre) share with the Basque Country a reputation for serving some of the finest food in the peninsula. Catalonia has so many dishes that it warrants a separate chapter; but Aragon and Navarre contribute many recipes to this section, notably those featuring the region's favorite ingredients—fish, seafood, and lamb.

The Mallos de Riglos rock formations form part of the foothills of the Pyrenees. Rugged terrain and spectacular natural beauty are par for the course in this part of Spain.

Asadilla
Baked salad of red pepper and tomato

*T*he name of this recipe means "little baked vegetables."
This vibrantly red salad is a Spanish summer favorite.
*Try serving it with lightly toasted crusty bread, or decorate
with strips of anchovy fillet.*

If you have gas, hold the peppers on a carving fork in the flame until black and blistered. Otherwise broil them, giving them a quarter turn every 5 minutes. Put them in a plastic bag for 10 minutes, then strip off the skins. Pull out the stems and discard the seeds, but keep the juice.

Meanwhile skin and quarter the tomatoes. Turn their seeds and juice into a small jug. Slice the flesh lengthwise into strips and put into an oiled baking dish. Slice the peppers the same way and mix in. Sprinkle with the garlic, marjoram, remaining oil, and salt and pepper. Press the tomato and pepper juices through a strainer, add them, and mix everything gently. Bake in an oven preheated to the highest possible temperature for about 20 minutes. Let cool and serve.

Ingredients
2 large red bell peppers
2 large ripe tomatoes
3 tbsp olive oil
2 garlic cloves, finely chopped
1 tbsp chopped fresh marjoram
salt and freshly ground black pepper

Serves 4

Piperada
Basque-style eggs

*P*iperada is a filling egg dish, which makes a delicious brunch, and it can also be served as a tapa. A popular variation of this recipe serves the piperada on toasted bread rounds dripping with butter. Either way, this simple egg dish is sure to become a part of your culinary repertoire.

Heat the oil in a skillet and sauté the onions, bell peppers, and garlic until tender. Fold in the ham and tomatoes, and season with salt and pepper. Continue to heat until the vegetables are almost cooked.

Lightly beat the eggs with a fork. Pour the eggs over the vegetables and cook over low heat until the eggs are thick but still soft. Garnish with parsley, and serve warm.

Ingredients

4 tbsp olive oil

2 small onions, peeled and finely diced

1 medium green bell pepper, seeded and
    sliced into thin strips

1 medium red bell pepper, seeded and sliced
    into thin strips

2 cloves garlic, peeled and minced

1 slice cured ham, cut into strips

2 large tomatoes, chopped

salt and pepper, to taste

4 eggs

chopped parsley, to garnish

Serves 2

Esparragos con dos salsas
White asparagus with two sauces

*W*hite asparagus is highly regarded in Spain. It is grown in
Navarre and transported from there across the whole of Spain.
You can use canned asparagus if you cannot obtain the fresh spears.

Drain the asparagus well and put it on a dish. For the vinaigrette, mix oil, vinegar, salt, and pepper together in a jug. For the tomato sauce, chop the tomato flesh into neat dice. Mix in the onion and parsley and season lightly with salt and either paprika or cayenne pepper.

To serve, arrange the tomato sauce in neat piles round the asparagus. Pass round the vinaigrette and allow everyone to pour their own. Eat the asparagus with one sauce, then the other.

Ingredients

14 oz asparagus, freshly cooked
4 fl. oz olive oil
3 tbsp wine vinegar
salt and freshly ground black pepper
2 ripe tomatoes, skinned and deseeded
1 tbsp chopped onion
1 tbsp chopped fresh parsley
pinch hot paprika or cayenne pepper

Serves 4

Berenjenas rellenas de hongros
Mushroom-stuffed eggplant

Ingredients

2 eggplants

2 small onions, chopped

2 tbsp olive oil

3 garlic cloves, finely chopped

7 oz mushrooms, cleaned and sliced

salt and freshly ground black pepper

2 oz Parmesan cheese, grated

Serves 4 as a starter

*E*ggplants were introduced to Spain by the Moors in the early Middle Ages. Since then they have been one of the peninsula's favorite vegetables.

Halve the eggplants lengthwise and remove the flesh carefully so that the skin is not broken. Reserve the skins and chop the flesh finely.

Meanwhile, fry the onions in the oil in a skillet until they begin to color. Put in the garlic and mushrooms and cook until they soften. Add the eggplant flesh and fry until golden, stirring occasionally. Season the eggplant skins and the flesh in the pan and then stuff the skins with the fried mixture.

Arrange the stuffed vegetables in a gratin dish and sprinkle with the cheese. Brown under a hot broiler for 5 minutes and serve.

Bacalao a la vizcaina
Salt cod in spicy tomato sauce

*S*alt cod is very popular in Mediterranean countries, where its delicate balance of salt and fish tastes is greatly admired—like caviar is elsewhere. You must soak the fish for 24 hours, or even longer if the fish is stiff as a board with a grayish tinge. Take out the best pieces to use in this exquisite dish; the rest can be saved for stews and salads.

Broil the red bell peppers, giving them a quarter turn every 5 minutes, until they are charred on all sides. Put them in a plastic bag for 10 minutes. Then skin and halve them, discarding stalks and seeds. Cut the flesh into strips. Soak the choricero peppers, if using, for 30 minutes. Put the drained salt cod in a large saucepan with the bay leaf and parsley stalks. Cover with water, bring to a boil, and remove immediately from the heat. Let cool.

Save some of the fish soaking liquid and remove any bones from the fish, but keep the skin. Blot the fish dry, then dust with flour and fry in very hot oil until golden. Reserve but do not try to keep the fish warm. Fry the onions in the same oil. Before they color, add the garlic cloves and chopped tomatoes. If you have choriceros, scrape the pulp from them and add it to the pan. Add the reserved fish liquid. If not using choriceros, add the tomato paste and cayenne pepper now. When the sauce looks thick, purée it in a blender. Taste for seasoning: a little lemon juice will make it spicier. On the other hand, if it is too spicy, the clear honey will subdue it.

Pour half the tomato sauce into an ovenproof dish and arrange the pieces of fish over it. Cover with the rest of the sauce and decorate with strips of red pepper.

Ingredients

4 portions of salt cod, soaked (see page 111)
2 red bell peppers
10 choricero peppers (optional)
1 bay leaf
4 parsley stalks
1½ tbsp flour
4 tbsp olive oil
12 oz onions, peeled and sliced
3 garlic cloves
2 large ripe tomatoes, skinned and seeded
1 tbsp tomato paste (optional)
pinch of cayenne pepper (optional)
1 tsp lemon juice (optional)
¼ tsp honey (optional)

Serves 4

Ensalada de bacalao
Salt cod salad

This intensely savory salad is very appetizing, combining salty flavors with a sharp dressing. A little salt cod goes a long way in this dish, as its flavor is quite strong.

Cover the fish with water and soak in a medium saucepan for 2 hours, changing the water after the first hour.

Drain the fish. Return to the saucepan with fresh water and bring to a boil, then simmer for 20 minutes. Remove the pan from the heat, drain the fish, and leave until cool enough to handle.

Flake the fish, being sure to discard all the skin and dark meat. Combine the flaked fish with the onion, olives, olive oil, and vinegar in a mixing bowl. Serve chilled, garnished with parsley and lemon wedges.

Ingredients

1 lb salt cod
1 medium white onion, diced
6 jumbo green olives, pitted
  and sliced
2½ fl. oz olive oil
2 tablespoons red wine vinegar
fresh parsley and lemon wedges, to garnish

Serves 4

Fritas de bacalao
Salt cod fritters

Ingredients

6 fl. oz milk

½ lb salt cod, soaked for 24 hours

1 large potato, peeled, cooked, and mashed

1 shallot, finely chopped

2 tbsp chopped fresh parsley

ground black pepper

juice of ½ lemon

2 tbsp all-purpose flour

1 egg, beaten

4 tbsp dry breadcrumbs

sunflower oil, for frying

4 fl. oz mayonnaise

1½ garlic cloves, crushed

1 tsp lemon juice

Serves 4

Try to avoid the drier end pieces of salt cod when making this dish—the tender middle section will give a more juicy and flavorful result. Remember to drain the cod and change the soaking water several times during its 24 hours of submersion.

Bring the milk to a simmer in a medium pan. Add the cod and poach gently for about 10 minutes, until the fish flakes easily. Remove any skin and bones, and flake the flesh into a bowl. Add the potatoes, shallot, and parsley, and mix well. Season with black pepper and add the lemon juice.

Shape the mixture into 8–12 patties, dust with flour, dip in beaten egg, then coat in breadcrumbs. Place on a platter or tray, cover, and chill for at least 30 minutes.

Meanwhile, combine the mayonnaise, garlic, and lemon juice, and add a grind of black pepper. Transfer to a bowl and set aside. Heat about 1 inch sunflower oil in a large pan. Add the patties in batches and fry for about 3 minutes on each side, until golden. Drain on paper towels and serve with the garlic mayonnaise.

Biscay Bay sole with cream and shellfish
Lenguada a la vizcaina

Ingredients

2 tbsp chopped onion

6 black peppercorns

4 tbsp chopped fresh parsley

1 bay leaf

7 fl. oz dry white wine

16 clams or mussels, cleaned

4 tbsp butter

4 sole fillets

1½ tbsp flour

salt and freshly ground pepper

4 fl. oz whipping cream

Serves 4

*S*ole are fished right through the Bay of Biscay, right down to the Basque coast. This type of old-fashioned cooking, with a rich sauce, has been popular for over a century. Shellfish make the perfect garnish, and cooked in this way they provide the stock for the dish.

Put the chopped onion in a saucepan with the peppercorns, 2 tablespoons of parsley, the bay leaf, and the wine. Bring to a simmer. Put in the clams or mussels, cover, and cook for 1–2 minutes until they open. Remove the shellfish, then let the liquid boil for 5 minutes and reserve. Take one shell off each mussel (discarding any that are still shut).

Melt the butter in a skillet. Dust the fish fillets in a seasoned flour and fry, 2 at a time, for a couple of minutes on each side. Remove to a warm serving plate and keep warm.

Add 1 teaspoon of flour to the pan and stir in the butter. Strain in the reserved shellfish stock, add the cream, and stir to deglaze the pan. Boil to reduce the sauce by half, adding the shellfish, face upward, to warm them. This sauce should need no seasoning, but taste to check. Pour it over the sole, sprinkle with parsley, and serve. Slim roasted leeks make a good accompaniment for this dish.

Sunset on San Juan de Gaztelugatxe, an island off the Bay of Biscay.

Patatas con sepias y almejas
Potatoes with cuttlefish, clams, and peppers

*T*his is a simple dish of potatoes in a green sauce, with a fresh sea flavor coming from the two kinds of shellfish. Cuttlefish are well suited to stewing as their tough flesh is softened by the long, slow cooking. Substitute a large squid if cuttlefish are unavailable.

Cut the tentacles off the cuttlefish or squid and separate them. Cut the body into thick strips. Put 2 tablespoons of oil in a large saucepan and fry the garlic cloves until they color. Remove at once to a mortar.

Add 2 more tablespoons of oil and fry the onion and ham over medium heat. When the onion starts to color, add the cuttlefish or squid and cook until the strips stiffen. Add the peppers and stir a couple of minutes. Pack in the potatoes and pour in a pint of water to barely cover. Season with salt and bring to a simmer.

Mash the garlic in the mortar to a paste, working in 2 tablespoons of parsley, the saffron, and the wine. Stir this, with some pepper, into the casserole. Cook until the potatoes are almost tender (about 20 minutes). Take off the lid halfway through, to evaporate some of the liquid.

Add the clams and simmer for 2 more minutes. Check the seasonings and sprinkle with the remaining parsley.

Ingredients
1 lb cuttlefish or squid, cleaned
4 tbsp olive oil
2 garlic cloves
1 onion, chopped
2 oz raw ham, diced
2 green bell peppers, seeded and cut into strips
2 lb potatoes, peeled and diced
salt and freshly ground black pepper
6 tbsp chopped fresh parsley
5 saffron strands
2 fl. oz white wine
1 lb clams, cleaned

Serves 4

Cuttlefish, clams, and other seafood on sale in a typically well-stocked Spanish fish market.

Chilindrón de cordero
Lamb and roasted pepper stew

*P*iquillo peppers are roasted and canned Spanish sweet peppers. *If you can't find them, substitute any roasted peppers.*

Coat the bottom of a large saucepan with olive oil and heat. Add the lamb and brown on all sides. Remove the lamb from the pan and add the onions, garlic, and ham. Cook until the vegetables become soft.

Add the piquillo peppers; deglaze the pan by adding the sherry, port, and white wine. Bring to a boil then reduce the heat and simmer until the mixture is reduced by half.

Return the lamb to the pan and add the tomatoes, bay leaf, and rosemary. Simmer for 3 hours and serve with boiled rice and red beans.

Ingredients

olive oil, for cooking

3-lb lamb shoulder

1 onion, peeled and chopped

4 garlic cloves, finely chopped

4 oz Serrano ham, sliced

1 cup drained piquillo peppers

7 fl. oz dry (fino) or semi-dry (amontillado) sherry

7 fl. oz ruby port

7 fl. oz dry white wine

10-oz can whole tomatoes

1 bay leaf

2 sprigs fresh rosemary

boiled rice and red beans, to serve

Serves 4

Alubias de Tolosa
Tolosa red bean stew with pork

*T*olosa, in the Basque Country, is famous for its kidney beans, which are long and as black as coal. Basques adore red beans, too, so use whichever red beans are available to you. The traditional dish contains the red chorizo sausage and the black morcilla, along with cured pork. This recipe can work equally well as a starter or tapa for 6.

Ingredients

1 lb red beans, soaked overnight

5 oz pork belly or boiling bacon, in one piece

1 large onion, finely chopped

4 tbsp olive oil

2 chorizo sausages

1 morcillo or 5 oz black pudding

1 large green bell pepper, seeded and chopped

salt and freshly ground black pepper

2 garlic cloves, finely chopped

Serves 4

Drain the beans and put them in a pan with the pork and half the chopped onion. Add 1 tablespoon of oil and cover with water. Bring to a boil, then turn down the heat, cover, and simmer gently for 2 hours or until the meat is tender. Watch that the water level remains high enough, adding more if necessary, but always in small quantities.

Heat the rest of the oil in a skillet. Slice and fry the chorizos and morcillo or black pudding with the chopped pepper.

Remove the pork or bacon from the beans and chop it into cubes. Check the amount of liquid in the beans: it should now be well reduced. If not, then pour some off. Add all the meats to the pan and season everything well.

Fry the remaining onion in the same pan used for the sausage, adding the garlic at the end. Stir into the beans and simmer for 10 minutes more.

Flan de naranjas
Orange flan

*A*lthough meals in Spain usually end with a piece of fresh fruit, Spaniards eagerly consume prepared desserts on special occasions or holidays. Flan, in particular, tops the list of Spanish dessert favorites. While most flans resemble traditional custard desserts, this flan is infused with a delicate orange flavor, a lingering reminder of Spain's Moorish past.

Preheat the oven to 350° F (180° C). To make the caramel topping, heat the sugar and the water in a small saucepan, swirling gently until a golden brown caramel is formed. Immediately divide the mixture evenly among four individual ramekins. Swirl and tilt the ramekins to ensure that the caramel coats the ramekins' sides and bases. Place the ramekins in a baking pan.

In a small bowl, bring the orange juice and orange rind to a boil, then remove from the heat. Meanwhile, in a separate bowl, whisk together the eggs and egg yolks with the remaining sugar, until the mixture is thick. Pour in the orange juice and rind, stirring constantly.

Divide this mixture among the four ramekins in the baking pan, then pour boiling water around them to create a bain-marie. Bake in the oven for about 25 minutes or until lightly set. Allow to cool, then refrigerate overnight.

Immediately before serving, briefly immerse the bases of the ramekins in hot water and, if necessary, pass a knife around the outer edges of the ramekins to make unmolding easier. Inverse and unmold the desserts onto serving saucers. Decorate with fresh orange slices or candied orange peel.

Ingredients
5 oz sugar, for the caramel topping
4 fl. oz water, for the caramel topping
15 fl. oz freshly squeezed orange juice
grated rind of 1 orange
4 medium eggs
2 medium egg yolks
5 oz sugar
orange slices or candied orange peel, to decorate

Serves 4

Intxaursalsa
Festive walnut cream

Ingredients
18 fl. oz milk
4½ oz sugar
strip **of lemon** zest
½ cinnamon stick
4½ oz shelled walnuts
1 slice stale bread, crusts removed and lightly toasted
3½ fl. oz light cream
ground cinnamon

Serves 4

*T*his chilled walnut cream is served as a dessert on festive occasions, especially Christmas Eve.

Bring the milk to a boil with the sugar, lemon zest, and cinnamon stick. Reduce the heat. Grind the walnuts in a food processor, being careful not to over-grind or they will turn oily. Add the ground nuts to the milk and simmer for 30 minutes.

Rub the bread into crumbs and add it to the pan. Simmer briefly, then remove the zest and cinnamon. Off the heat, beat with a wooden spoon or purée in a food processor. Stir in the cream, return to the heat, and simmer gently for 2–3 more minutes.

Chill well and serve very cold, lightly dusted with cinnamon.

CHAPTER 4

Catalonia

Catalonia, in the north-eastern corner of Spain, is home to some 7 million people who consider themselves to be a people apart from the rest of the country. They are recognized as being largely autonomous, and their culture and language are quite distinct. Catalonia today is a dynamic region whose capital Barcelona, in particular, is proud of its individual character. Just as distinctive is the regional cuisine, based around simple staples such as toasted bread, rubbed with olive oil and spread with tomatoes. Understandably in a coastal region, the fish and shellfish are excellent. Meat is often combined with seafood in a style of cooking called mar i muntanya— the sea and the mountains.

La Boqueria market, with its vast array of produce, has been at the center of Barcelona's shopping culture since it opened in the nineteenth century. There has been a market on this site, just off La Rambla, for 800 years.

Escalivada
Roasted vegetable salad

*F*rom the Catalan verb escalivar, meaning "to cook over hot embers," escalivada is a colorful array of vegetables, roasted to perfection and glistening with olive oil. Escalivada is usually served on a rustic, earthenware platter, and, as with most tapas, should be accompanied by thick slices of fresh crusty bread.

Lay the onions on a baking sheet and bake in the oven at 350°F (180°C) for 10 minutes. Add the eggplant and bake for a further 10 minutes. Add the bell peppers, tomatoes, and half of the garlic cloves and bake until all vegetables are tender. Remove the vegetables from the oven and allow to cool.

Peel the vegetables with your fingers. Cut the eggplants into strips. Remove the stem, core, and seeds from the bell peppers, and cut into strips as well. Seed the tomatoes, then slice into wedges. Thinly slice the onion. Arrange the vegetables attractively on a serving platter.

In a food processor, combine the roasted garlic, the remaining cloves of raw garlic, the cumin seeds, lemon juice, vinegar, olive oil, sweet paprika, and rosemary. When the mixture is smooth and homogenized, pour it evenly over the vegetables. Season with salt and serve.

Ingredients

2 medium yellow onions, unpeeled
1 medium eggplant
1 large green bell pepper
1 large red bell pepper
1 large yellow bell pepper
2 medium tomatoes
8 cloves garlic
2 tsp cumin seeds
2 tbsp lemon juice
3 tbsp sherry vinegar
4 tbsp olive oil
1 tsp sweet paprika
1 tsp chopped fresh rosemary
salt, to taste

Serves 4

Xató
Frisée salad with cured fish

Ingredients

3½ oz soaked salt cod

1 head frisée or escarole

2-oz can anchovies, drained

1 tbsp olive oil

1 tbsp sherry vinegar

4 tbsp romesco sauce (see page 138)

4-oz can tuna, drained and flaked

2 handfuls small green olives

Serves 6

*S*pain produces a bigger range of cured fish than any other country round the Mediterranean. Here three of the common ones are combined with crisp green leaves and a sophisticated dressing of hazelnuts and chiles. The dish is pronounced the way "chateau" is said in English. The cod must be free of all skin and bones and soaked to the point where it is not completely desalinated—so it is poised at the appetizing point between being salted and fresh.

Separate the frisée or escarole leaves, wash them, dry well, and chill. Drain the cod and pat dry with paper towel. Pull the flesh apart into flakes and small strips. Cut the anchovy fillets into small pieces on the diagonal.

Put the frisée in a big, shallow salad bowl. Stir the oil and sherry vinegar into the romesco sauce and check the seasonings—it should be distinctly piquant. Spoon the sauce over the salad, and toss until it is well distributed.

Add the salt cod and the tuna, separated into its natural flakes, and toss again. Serve on individual plates, distributing the anchovy fillets and olives evenly over the leaves.

Espinacas Catalanas
Catalan-style spinach with raisins and pine nuts

*S*weet, plump raisins and crisp pine nuts are often paired together *in classic Catalan cuisine. Try them tossed with fresh spinach and stuffed olives. This traditional combination is excellent as a tapa or as a side dish. As a variation, omit the croutons and serve the spinach on toasted bread slices.*

Heat the olive oil in a skillet. Add the garlic and onion and fry until golden. Set aside.

Rinse the spinach and trim the leaves from the stalks. Discard the stalks. Place the spinach in a large saucepan, cover, and cook over low heat for 10 minutes in the water clinging to its leaves. Drain, then stir the spinach into the onion and garlic. Mix in the raisins, pine nuts, and olives. Season generously with salt and pepper. Transfer to a serving dish, sprinkle croutons on top, and serve warm.

Ingredients
3 tbsp olive oil
2 cloves garlic, finely chopped
1 medium onion, finely chopped
2 lb spinach
2½ oz raisins, soaked in hot water for
    20 minutes and drained
4 tbsp pine nuts
2 oz pimento-stuffed olives, finely chopped
salt and pepper, to taste
croutons, to serve

Serves 4–6

Paella esmeralda
Emerald paella

*B*ased on Catalonia's spinach with raisins and pine nuts (page 130), this vegetable paella owes its name to the generous use of green bell peppers, parsley, olives, and spinach that flavor the rice. This paella can include raisins too, if you like. Although not a traditional accompaniment to paella, they can add an unexpected and welcome sweetness to the saffron-enhanced rice.

Combine the vegetable broth, parsley, basil, saffron, and cumin in a skillet and heat over low heat. Set aside.

Heat the olive oil in the paella pan and lightly toast the pine nuts. Add the onion, garlic, and bell pepper and sauté until tender. Add the olives and the spinach and cook for several minutes, until the spinach has wilted.

Mix in the rice and pour in the warm vegetable broth, combining well. Cook until the rice is tender and all the broth has been absorbed, about 25 minutes. Mix in the cheese, and allow to cool for several minutes before serving.

Ingredients
1½ pints vegetable broth
1½ tbsp chopped fresh parsley
1 tsp dried basil
½ tsp saffron
¼ tsp ground cumin
3 fl. oz olive oil
4 tbsp pine nuts
1 large onion, finely chopped
8 cloves garlic, finely chopped
1 medium green bell pepper, finely chopped
6 oz pimento-stuffed olives, chopped
10 oz spinach leaves, destemmed and chopped
12 oz paella rice
1½ oz grated Manchego or Parmesan cheese

Serves 6

Paella de rape a la Catalana
Catalan-style paella with monkfish

*T*his paella features monkfish, which has gained in popularity in recent years. Prepared and cooked correctly, monkfish looks and tastes much like lobster. Here, the subtle flavor and tenderness of the monkfish add the perfect accents to the plump, juicy rice. A chilled white wine is an ideal accompaniment to this seafood paella.

Heat 6 fl. oz of the olive oil in a paella pan over medium to high heat. Lightly fry the monkfish pieces all over in the oil and transfer to a platter.

In the same oil, sauté the chile and transfer to a mortar. Fry the slice of bread in the same oil until golden and transfer to the mortar with the chile. Mash together until a paste is formed.

Add the chopped garlic and tomatoes to the paella pan and sauté for several minutes. Pour in the remaining oil and, when sufficiently heated, add the rice. Place the monkfish pieces on top, and add the broth, mashed chile and bread, and the saffron. Cook for 20–25 minutes, or until the liquid has been absorbed and the rice is tender.

Season with salt and pepper and serve immediately.

Ingredients

8 fl. oz olive oil

1½ lb monkfish, cut into pieces

1 small fresh chile pepper

1 slice white bread

5 cloves garlic, finely chopped

2 medium tomatoes, skinned, seeded, and
  chopped

1 lb paella rice

2 pints fish or chicken broth

¼ tsp saffron

Salt and pepper, to taste

Serves 6

Zarzuela
Fish stew

*T*he name zarzuela—literally a light, whimsical operetta—
perfectly reflects the bright colors and vibrancy of this
unforgettable feast of fish. This dish should be served with fresh
crusty bread to mop up the delicious juices.

Heat the oil in a large pan and cook the onion and garlic until tender. Add the tomatoes, bay leaf, oregano, and saffron. Cook for about 10 minutes, stirring occasionally. Increase the heat to high and add the monkfish, clam juice, wine, and parsley. Bring to a boil, then add the clams, mussels, shrimp, and squid. Reduce the heat to medium, cover and cook for about a further 10 minutes.

Discard any mussels and clams that have failed to open. Remove and discard the bay leaf. Season with salt and pepper, transfer to an earthenware serving bowl, and garnish with chopped parsley. Serve immediately, with crusty bread.

Ingredients

4 fl. oz olive oil
1 medium onion, peeled and chopped
2 cloves garlic, finely chopped
2 medium tomatoes, skinned, seeded, and diced
1 bay leaf
¼ tsp oregano
¼ tsp saffron
8 oz monkfish, skinned and cut into chunks
16 fl. oz clam juice
4 fl. oz dry white wine
1 tbsp chopped parsley
12 clams, scrubbed
12 mussels, scrubbed and debearded
8 oz shrimp, peeled and deveined
8 oz squid, cleaned and sliced into rings
salt and pepper, to taste
chopped parsley, to garnish

Serves 4

Langosta a la Catalana
Catalan-style lobster

Ingredients

4 oz finely sliced Serrano or Parma ham

2 canned red pimientos, drained

4 tbsp Spanish olive oil

1 medium onion, finely chopped

2 cloves garlic, finely chopped

12 oz canned crushed tomatoes

4 fl. oz dry white wine

4 small cooked lobsters

4 tbsp brandy

salt and freshly ground black pepper

2 tbsp chopped fresh parsley

chopped fresh parsley and lemon wedges,
   to garnish

Serves 4

If lobster is too expensive, this dish works just as well with large shrimp. Rich and delicious, this lobster goes well with a crisp salad and rice, or some bread, to mop up the sauce.

Cut the ham and pimientos into thin strips. Heat the olive oil in a frying pan and gently fry the onion and garlic for 5 minutes until softened. Add the ham and cook, stirring, for a further 2 minutes.

Add the pimientos, tomatoes, and wine, bring to a boil, and simmer, uncovered, for 15 minutes or until thickened.

Meanwhile, wash and pat dry the lobsters and cut in half lengthwise. Add the lobsters to the sauce, making sure they are completely submerged. Add the brandy, seasoning, and parsley and heat through gently for 4–5 minutes.

Pile on to warm serving plates, garnish with some parsley, and serve with the wedges of lemon to squeeze over.

Pescado con salsa romesco
Flat fish with hazelnut and chile sauce

Small flat fish, simply fried, are a flavorful treat—especially when moist and slightly underdone. The sauce, salsa romesco, is a famous and sophisticated Catalan favorite.

Start the sauce by toasting the nuts in a low oven (320°F/120°C) for 20 minutes until biscuit-colored. Fry the garlic, then the bread slice, in 4 tablespoons olive oil, and reserve. Add the chopped tomato and chile or cayenne pepper to the pan and cook, stirring, until the mixture has thickened. Season with salt and pepper.

Grind the nuts in a blender. Add the bread, garlic, vinegar, and fino sherry and pulverize everything. Stir this into the tomato sauce. Check the seasoning.

Dust the sole with seasoned flour. Heat the butter and oil in a skillet. When very hot, put in the fish. Whole fish need 3–4 minutes for the first side, 2 minutes for the second. If using fillets, allow about 2 minutes each side.

Serve on hot plates and pass the sauce round in a bowl.

Ingredients

1 oz blanched hazelnuts
2 garlic cloves, finely chopped
4–6 tbsp olive oil
1 slice stale bread
1 large ripe tomato, skinned and seeded
½ dried chile or a pinch of cayenne pepper
salt and freshly ground black pepper
2 tsp red wine vinegar
4 tbsp fino sherry
4 small lemon sole or other flatfish, cleaned
2 tbsp flour
salt and pepper
2 tbsp butter
1 tbsp olive oil

Serves 4

Costa Brava shoreline near Lloret de Mar, Catalonia.

Porc amb musclos
Pork with mussels

Ingredients
1¾ lb lean pork, cubed
salt and freshly ground black pepper
2 tbsp lard
2 tbsp olive oil
1½ lb onions, chopped
6 garlic cloves, finely chopped
12-oz can tomatoes
1 tbsp paprika
½ dried chile, seeded and chopped
2 bay leaves
1 strip dried or 2 strips fresh orange peel
3 lb mussels, cleaned
7 fl. oz dry white wine
6 tbsp chopped fresh parsley

Serves 8

So-called "sea and mountain" dishes like this one were originally an economical way of eking out small quantities. Later they became more lavish, with combinations like chicken and lobster.

Heat the lard in a wide saucepan. Season the pork well and fry in the melted lard until it is golden on all sides. Remove from the pan. Add the oil and chopped onions and cook gently until soft. Add the garlic, tomatoes (breaking them up with a spoon), paprika, chile, bay leaves, and orange peel. Cook for 20 minutes until reduced.

Meanwhile put the mussels in a big saucepan over medium heat until they open. Then remove. Put in the wine and 2 tablespoons of parsley. Add half the shellfish and cover tightly. Steam for 4 minutes, shaking the pan occasionally if they are not all in one layer. Remove the first batch of mussels from the pan and cook the second batch. Remove the top shells from each mussel and throw away any mussels that smell strongly or remain shut.

Add the pork and the mussel liquor to the sauce and simmer for 30 minutes, until the meat is tender and the sauce is reduced. Check the seasoning, add the mussels, and warm through. Sprinkle with parsley and serve.

A wide range of pork products are enjoyed across Spain. A distinctively Catalonian touch is to combine them with seafood.

Crema Catalana
Sweet Catalan cream

*B*ecause of its crisp, caramelized topping, this creamy Catalan *dessert is often compared to the French crème brûlée. Sweet Catalan cream, however, is not as heavy or rich as its French cousin, and thus makes a more pleasant ending to a heavy dinner.*

In a saucepan, bring the milk, cinnamon stick, lemon rind, and vanilla extract to a boil. Simmer for several minutes then discard the cinnamon stick and lemon rind. Set the flavored milk aside.

In a bowl, whisk the egg yolks together with the cornstarch and 5 ounces of the sugar until the mixture is creamy. Gradually pour this mixture into the saucepan with the milk, mixing continuously.

Slowly heat the mixture until it begins to thicken, taking care that the mixture does not boil. Pour into four shallow, heatproof serving dishes, allow to cool, and refrigerate for several hours.

Immediately before serving, preheat the broiler and scatter the remaining sugar evenly over each serving. Place the dishes under the broiler until the sugar topping begins to caramelize. Remove from the broiler and serve.

Ingredients
15 fl. oz milk
1 cinnamon stick
rind of 1 lemon
1 tsp vanilla extract
4 medium egg yolks
1 tbsp cornstarch
7 oz superfine sugar

Serves 4

CHAPTER 5

Eastern Spain

T he east of Spain is perhaps most famous for its fine beaches, especially the tourist-oriented coasts of the Balearic Islands. But the cuisine of these provinces also earns them renown; Valencia is known worldwide for its oranges and its rice fields. Paella was created here two centuries ago, and there are now scores of versions as well as many other rice dishes. The east coast also has Alicante, with its date palms and African climate, and Murcia, which remained under Arab rule until the seventeenth century.

The fort of Dénia overlooking this small coastal town in Alicante province.

Tumbet
Eggplant casserole

Tumbet, the traditional eggplant dish of the Balearic Islands, can stand on its own as a main course, or can be served as an accompaniment to heartier meat dishes. While many chefs choose to serve tumbet fresh from the oven, this dish is also delectable when left to cool and eaten at room temperature.

Leave the eggplant slices in a colander for 1 hour. Blot with paper towels.

Heat the olive oil in a skillet over low heat. Fry the potato slices until golden. Lay the potato slices along the bottom of a heatproof casserole dish and season with salt and pepper. In the same oil, lightly fry the eggplant slices. Transfer to the casserole and layer the eggplant on top of the potato slices. Fry the bell peppers in the same oil, transfer to the casserole, and arrange them on top of the eggplant. Fry the zucchini in the same oil. Transfer to the casserole dish and layer over the bell peppers. Sprinkle with salt and pepper.

Fry the minced garlic in the same skillet, adding more oil if necessary, until golden. Mix in the chopped tomatoes, and cook over medium heat for about 20 minutes.

Pass the tomato sauce through a sieve, sprinkle with sugar, and pour over the vegetables in the casserole. Transfer to a 350°F (180°C) oven and bake for about 10 minutes. The eggplant casserole can be served hot or at room temperature.

Ingredients

3 medium eggplants, cut into ¼-inch slices and sprinkled with salt
8 fl. oz olive oil
2 large potatoes, sliced thin
salt and pepper, to taste
2 small red bell peppers, chopped
3 small zucchini, sliced
3 cloves garlic, minced
2 large tomatoes, skinned, seeded, and chopped
pinch of sugar

Serves 4

Bajoques farcides
Baked peppers with rice stuffing

Ingredients

3 tbsp olive oil

1 large chicken breast, diced

5 oz lean pork, diced

4 oz ham or smoked bacon, diced

7 oz short-grain rice

2 garlic cloves, finely chopped

2 lb ripe tomatoes, skinned, seeded and
   chopped

1 green bell pepper, finely chopped

3 tbsp corn kernels

2 tsp paprika

pinch powdered saffron

salt and freshly ground black pepper

6 tbsp chopped fresh parsley

6 large red bell peppers

Serves 6

The title of this recipe is the Valencian dialect name for rice-stuffed peppers. This delicate version comes from Alcoy.

Heat the oil in a large saucepan and fry the chicken, pork, and ham or bacon until colored on all sides. Take the pan off the heat and reserve.

Meanwhile, cook the rice in plenty of boiling salted water until done—usually about 15 minutes, but follow the instructions on the package. Drain and reserve the rice.

Add the garlic, chopped tomatoes, green bell pepper, corn kernels, paprika, saffron, salt and pepper, and parsley to the pan containing the meat. Let the sauce simmer and reduce the volume of liquid by about half. Stir the rice into the sauce.

Oil a deep ovenproof dish big enough to take all the peppers. Cut off "lids" at the stalk ends of the peppers and remove the seeds. Stuff them with the meat and rice mixture and replace the lids. Tuck the peppers into the dish, cover with foil, and bake at 325°F (170°C) for 1¼ hours.

Zarangollo
Zucchini and onion hash

This is a very traditional dish, still eaten in the same way as it was before the introduction of American vegetables to Spain. After Columbus's voyage, peppers and tomatoes were added to this base to make pisto and ratatouille. The onions are softened in oil, then the vegetables cook in their own juices. Sometimes, to make the dish more substantial, eggs are scrambled in.

Ingredients
2 fl oz olive oil
1 onion, peeled and finely sliced
2 garlic cloves, finely chopped
2 lb zucchini, peeled and finely sliced
salt and freshly ground black pepper
½ tbsp chopped fresh oregano
fried bread to serve

Serves 2–4

Put the oil in a heavy-based saucepan and add the onion. Cook very slowly for about 10 minutes, adding the garlic as the onion begins to soften. Add the zucchini and season with salt and pepper. Stir gently for a couple of minutes. Cover with foil and the saucepan lid and cook over low heat for 30 minutes.

Stir, breaking up the zucchini with a wooden spoon. Add the oregano, re-cover the pot, and cook slowly for another 30 minutes, until everything is soft and amalgamated. Take the lid off for the last 10 minutes, to allow some of the juices to evaporate.

Serve with fried bread.

Ensalada Murciana
Murcian salad of mixed baked vegetables

Ingredients
1 lb 4 oz eggplant
3 green bell peppers
4 medium onions, peeled
4 large tomatoes
1 bunch scallions, trimmed
8 tbsp olive oil
3 garlic cloves, bruised
juice of 1 lemon
salt and freshly ground black pepper
4 tbsp chopped fresh parsley

Serves 4 as a main course

*L*ike the Catalan escalivada (page 126), the vegetables used to make this salad are baked round the barbecue in summer, then dressed to serve cold. Here they are baked in the oven and make a good vegetarian main course. You could alter the selection of vegetables—just modify cooking times to suit them.

Preheat the oven to 400˚F (200˚C). Put the eggplant, peppers, onions, tomatoes, and scallions into a large ovenproof dish with the oil and garlic cloves. Also add 5 tablespoons cold water to stop the juices burning. Bake the vegetables for 25 minutes, then remove the tomatoes. After another 15 minutes, remove the peppers. Give the other vegetables a squeeze to see how close they are to being done. Put the peppers in a plastic bag; this helps with the skinning later. The eggplant will probably be ready in about another 15 minutes, but onions usually need another 15 minutes or more. Stir the juices in the dish and pour them into a cup, discarding the garlic cloves.

Skin the tomatoes and arrange them in the center of a big platter, then just cut them across like a star. Skin the rest of the vegetables, slice them lengthwise, and keep all the juices they exude. Arrange the vegetables in sets on the platter, radiating round the tomatoes. Sprinkle lemon juice over the salad and season. Then stir the reserved pan juices and dribble some into the center of the tomatoes and over the salad. Sprinkle with parsley and serve.

Palm trees and waterfall in Elche Murcia, Spain.

Paella mixta
Seafood, sausage, and chicken paella

This is the recipe that springs to mind when most people think of paella. While Valencia, the homeland of paella, rarely produces a paella mixing seafood with meat, this paella has caught the popular imagination outside Spain and tends to be the paella served in most Spanish-themed restaurants. It is easy to understand why few could resist the combination of delicate lobster meat, mussels, clams, and shrimp teamed with rich chorizo sausage and tender chicken.

Scrub and debeard the mussels and clams, discarding any that do not close when tapped sharply. Set aside.

Heat 2 fl. oz of the olive oil in a skillet. Add the pork, and brown on all sides. Mix in the garlic, onions, tomato, and bell peppers, stirring constantly until cooked. Remove from the pan and set aside.

In the same skillet, heat a further 2 fl. oz olive oil and cook the chicken until browned on all sides. Season with salt, pepper, paprika, rosemary, thyme, and cumin. Transfer the chicken to a plate and set aside. In the same skillet, cook the lobster claws over high heat for several minutes until the shells turn pink. Transfer to a plate and set aside.

Preheat the oven to 400°F (200°C). Heat 4 tablespoons olive oil in the skillet, and sauté the rice until it is translucent. Pour in the chicken broth, and combine well. Add the pork mixture, stirring constantly. Sprinkle in the saffron and continue to stir until well mixed.

Transfer the rice into a paella pan. Mix in the lobster, chicken, sausage, clams, mussels, shrimp, peas, and capers, combining well. Bake the paella, uncovered, and on the lowest oven shelf, for around 25 minutes, or until all the liquid has been absorbed.

Discard any mussels and clams that have failed to open. Serve the paella straight from the pan, garnished with lemon wedges.

Ingredients
10 mussels
10 clams
4 fl. oz, plus 4 tbsp, olive oil
2 oz boneless pork, diced
2 tsp minced garlic
6 oz onions, chopped fine
1 medium tomato, skinned, seeded, and chopped
1 small red bell pepper, seeded and cut into thin strips
1 small green bell pepper, seeded and cut into thin strips
1 small yellow bell pepper, seeded and cut into thin strips
2 lb skinless, boneless chicken breasts, cut into chunks
salt and pepper, to taste
1 tsp paprika
½ tsp dried rosemary
½ tsp dried thyme
¼ tsp ground cumin
1½ lb lobster claws
1½ lb paella rice
2 pints chicken broth
¼ tsp saffron
2 chorizo sausages, cooked and cut into chunks
10 uncooked shrimp, peeled and deveined
4 oz peas
4 tbsp capers
lemon wedges, to garnish

Serves 6

Paella de pollo, calabacines y romero
Paella with chicken, zucchini, and rosemary

Ingredients

6 fl. oz olive oil

3 lb chicken breasts, boned and cut into pieces

1 large onion, chopped

5 cloves garlic, minced

1 large green bell pepper, chopped

3 fl. oz dry sherry

12 oz paella rice

1¼ pints chicken broth

¼ tsp saffron

¼ tsp turmeric

3 tbsp chopped fresh rosemary

3 large zucchini, cut into 1½-inch strips

salt and freshly ground black pepper

Serves 6

*T*his deliciously flavored rice dish features tender chicken breasts subtly seasoned with fresh rosemary. It could be said that this paella brings good fortune to those who eat it, for, according to an ancient Spanish superstition, anyone who passes a rosemary bush must pull some sprigs off the fragrant shrub and pocket them to ensure good luck in the week to come. A touch of dry sherry lends this paella extra Andalusian flair.

Heat 2 fl. oz of the oil in a paella pan. Add the chicken and cook until done and browned on all sides. Set aside.

Clean the pan and heat the remaining olive oil over medium heat. Add the onion, and cook for 5 minutes. Add the garlic and green bell pepper and cook for 3 minutes. Add the sherry and cook for a further 1 minute. Pour in the rice and sauté for 5 minutes. Mix in the broth, saffron, turmeric, browned chicken, and 1½ tablespoons of the rosemary and cook for 15 minutes.

Sprinkle in the remaining rosemary and stir. Arrange the zucchini over the rice, cover, and cook for a further 10 minutes or until the rice and chicken are tender, and the broth has been absorbed. Allow to cool for 5 minutes, and serve.

Paella de gambas con Jerez
Shrimp paella with sherry

*T*he use of sherry in this dish evokes the taste of a paella served outdoors in a seaside restaurant. If you wish, lay lemon wedges around the edge of the rice for an even more attractive presentation.

Heat the oil in a paella pan over medium heat. Add the onions and garlic and sauté for about 5 minutes, or until onion is soft. Add the bell peppers and cook for about 5 minutes longer. Add the tomatoes and continue to cook for a further 8–10 minutes.

Add the rice and cook, stirring, for a further 5 minutes. Mix in the broth, sherry, shrimp, saffron, and salt and pepper. Bring to a simmer and cook gently for 20 minutes.

Boil the sliced carrots in salted water until almost tender. About 2 minutes before they are ready, add the scallions and sugarsnap peas and blanch briefly. Drain.

Arrange the carrots, scallions, and sugarsnap peas on top of the rice and continue cooking until all liquid has been absorbed and the rice is tender, about 5 minutes.

Ingredients

2 fl. oz olive oil

2 medium onions, chopped

5 cloves garlic, minced

1 small green bell pepper, diced

1 small red bell pepper, diced

3 large tomatoes, skinned, seeded, and chopped

12 oz paella rice

1 pint fish broth

8 fl. oz sherry

12 oz medium shrimp, peeled and deveined

½ tsp saffron

salt and pepper, to taste

3 medium carrots, peeled and sliced lengthwise

6 scallions, trimmed

3 oz sugarsnap peas, halved lengthwise

Serves 6

Paella vegetariana
Vegetarian paella

Ingredients

2 fl. oz olive oil

1 large yellow onion, chopped

5 cloves garlic, minced

1¾ pints vegetable broth

1 lb rice

1 small red bell pepper, cut into strips

1 small green bell pepper, cut into strips

1 small yellow bell pepper, cut into strips

4 medium tomatoes, seeded and chopped

4 oz frozen peas, defrosted

14 oz artichoke hearts, tough outer leaves
removed, and quartered

1 lemon

Serves 6

*T*his paella is so moist, full of flavor, and substantial, that you will scarcely notice it is meat-free. The green, red, and yellow bell peppers add a vibrant splash of color to the pale rice, while the tangy artichoke hearts, delicate peas, and juicy tomatoes ensure that this vegetarian meal will satisfy even the most avid carnivores.

Heat the oil in a paella pan and sauté the onion and garlic until the onion is tender and translucent. At the same time, heat the broth in a separate saucepan until simmering.

Pour the rice into the paella pan and sauté for about 3 minutes. Add the bell peppers and tomatoes and cook for a further 3 minutes. Add the simmering vegetable broth and cook over medium heat for 20 minutes or until almost tender and almost all the liquid has been absorbed. Stir in the peas.

Sprinkle the artichoke hearts with a few drops of lemon juice and arrange over the rice in an attractive pattern. Continue cooking until the liquid has been absorbed and the rice is tender. Garnish with lemon wedges and serve.

Paella de pollo y tomates secos

Chicken paella with sun-dried tomatoes

In this sophisticated paella, sun-dried tomatoes are enhanced by the flavor of dry sherry, and provide a flavorful contrast to the plump rice. Likewise, the interplay of mushrooms, onion, and garlic lends the paella a distinct pungency that is perfectly counterbalanced by the tender chicken. The delicate balance of flavors and simple preparation make this the perfect choice for a paella supper anytime.

Soak the chopped sun-dried tomatoes in the sherry for 30 minutes, then drain when ready to use.

Heat the olive oil in a paella pan over medium heat. Add the chicken and fry until browned on all sides.

Meanwhile, in a small saucepan over low heat, cook the mushrooms, onion, and garlic in 3 tablespoons sherry until the mushrooms are tender. Add this mixture to the paella pan and stir well. Mix in the sun-dried tomatoes and cook for 3 minutes. Pour in the rice and cook for a further 5 minutes, stirring frequently. Add the broth, saffron, and basil and cook for about 25 minutes, or until the rice and chicken are tender and the broth has been absorbed. Serve at once.

Ingredients

1 oz sun-dried tomatoes (not packed in olive oil), chopped

6 fl. oz dry sherry, for soaking

4 fl. oz olive oil

1½ lb skinless, boneless chicken breasts, cut into chunks

2½ oz sliced mushrooms

½ medium onion, finely chopped

3 cloves garlic, finely chopped

3 tbsp dry sherry

12 oz rice

1½ pints chicken broth

¼ tsp saffron

1 tsp dried basil

Serves 6

Paella con pasas y almendras tostadas
Paella with currants and toasted almonds

Ingredients

2 tbsp olive oil

2 medium onions, diced

4 cloves garlic, minced

12 oz skinless, boneless chicken breasts, cut into small chunks and seasoned with salt and pepper

1½ pints chicken broth

½ tsp saffron

12 oz paella rice

8 oz currants

handful of fresh cilantro, chopped

salt and pepper, to taste

2½ oz slivered almonds, toasted

Serves 6

This unusual recipe, combining chicken with currants and toasted almonds, produces a crisp and succulent rice with just a tinge of sweetness. If you do not have currants on hand, use raisins as a substitute.

Heat the oil in a paella pan over medium heat. Add the onion and garlic and sauté until tender. Add the chicken and cook until lightly browned on all sides, about 5 minutes.

At the same time, heat the chicken broth in a small skillet over low heat. Add the saffron, stir, and keep over low heat until ready for use.

Add the rice to the paella pan. Pour in the broth and reduce the heat to low. Cook until the broth has been absorbed and the rice is tender. Remove from the heat and mix in the currants and cilantro. Season with salt and pepper, sprinkle with the sliced toasted almonds, and serve.

Trempo
Balearic garden salad

*T*his pretty, fresh salad includes fruit and the local capers, which grow on the Balearic hillsides and are sold pickled to the whole of Spain.

Slice the tomatoes and peppers into rings. Line a big plate or shallow salad bowl with the tomato slices. Beat together the oil, vinegar, salt, and pepper in a bowl and put the pear and apple slices into this as they are ready, turning them to coat in the dressing (otherwise they will discolor). Arrange these over the tomatoes. Arrange the pepper rings on top and sprinkle with the scallions. Tuck bunches of purslane or watercress round the plate and in between the tomato. Dot with pieces of crumbled crackers and capers, and sprinkle with the remaining vinaigrette.

Ingredients
3 ripe tomatoes
2 green bell peppers, seeded
3 tbsp olive oil
2 tbsp vinegar
pinch of salt
freshly ground black pepper
1 ripe pear, peeled, cored, and sliced
1 apple, cored and sliced
2 scallions, chopped
small bunch purslane or watercress
2 crackers
3 tbsp capers

Serves 4

Coca enramada
Pizza with garden vegetables

*C*ocas are quicker than to make the Italian pizza and contain no cheese. They are at root a peasant dish—but the combination of bread, vegetables, and olive oil is delicious when the coca is enjoyed straight from the oven.

First make the pizza dough. Warm the milk to blood heat. Sift the flour into a food processor or big bowl and scatter with the salt. Add the dried yeast and 2 tablespoons of the oil to the bowl and work in enough of the warm milk to make a dough. If using a food processor, beat for 3–4 minutes, stopping every minute to break the dough up. Or turn the dough out onto a floured surface and knead it, pushing it out with the heel of one hand to a tongue shape, then folding and slapping it into a mound again. Do this until it becomes elastic. Shape the dough into a ball, put into an oiled bowl, cover with a cloth, and leave in a warm place for 30 minutes, or a refrigerator for several hours. Preheat the oven to 425°F (220°C). Meanwhile sauté the onion in 3 tablespoons of oil.

When the dough has doubled in size, put it in the middle of an oiled 12-inch pizza plate or baking sheet. Press it down with your knuckles to fit the plate with a slight rim round the outside. Oil the edges of the dough and spread the onion over the dough. Distribute the peppers and tomato over the top and season with salt and pepper. Dribble another tablespoon of oil over the top. Bake for 25–30 minutes.

Ingredients

5–6 fl. oz milk

9 oz strong all-purpose flour, plus extra for kneading

1 tsp salt

1½ tsp dried yeast

6 tbsp olive oil, plus extra

1 onion, finely chopped

2 small green bell peppers, seeded and chopped

1 large ripe tomato, skinned and seeded

salt and freshly ground black pepper

Serves 4

Flaò
Sweet cheesecake with mint

Ingredients

6 oz all-purpose flour, plus extra for rolling
pinch of salt
2 oz chilled butter, diced, plus extra for
  greasing
5 small eggs
1 tbsp aniseed liqueur
1 tbsp milk
3 tbsp honey
5 oz superfine sugar
14 oz full-fat cream cheese
15 fresh mint leaves
confectioner's sugar for dusting

Serves 8

*T*his is a very old recipe that appeared in the first cookbook printed in Spain, at the end of the fifteenth century. The cake is still made in Ibiza, especially at Easter time.

First make the pastry. Sift the flour and salt into a food processor or bowl. Cut in the fat, then beat in 1 egg and the aniseed liqueur, adding enough milk to help form a dough. Pull the pastry together into a ball and chill for 15 minutes.

Heat the oven to 325°F (170°C) with a heavy baking sheet in it to warm. Make the filling by beating the eggs, sugar, and honey together. Work in the cream cheese and mint leaves.

Roll out the pastry on a floured surface. Roll it round a rolling pin and lift this over a greased cake pan 10 inches in diameter. Fit the pastry into the pan. Pour in the filling, smooth the top, and bake on the baking sheet for 40–50 minutes, until slightly risen and golden on top.

Leave it to cool for 5 minutes, then remove from the pan. Chill well. Dust with confectioner's sugar before serving.

Ensaimadas
Majorcan sweet bread

A Majorcan favorite, ensaimadas are warm, yeast-based cakes fashioned into round, coiled shapes. Although delicious, these cakes are time-consuming to prepare, because the dough must be allowed to rise several times. Nevertheless, when time is available, these make delightful breakfast rolls. This recipe yields one very large, beautiful coil that can be sliced into individual portions. Serve with hot chocolate or steaming coffee.

Dissolve the yeast in the warmed milk and set aside.

Combine the sugar and salt together in a large bowl. Gradually add the flour and warm milk mixture. Blend thoroughly. Add the eggs and olive oil, mix well, and knead until soft and well-blended. Cover with a damp cloth and leave to rise in a warm place for about 1 hour, or until the dough has doubled in volume.

Knead the dough again, and using a rolling pin, roll the dough as thin as possible over a floured surface. Brush the entire surface of the dough with softened butter.

Start rolling the dough, bit by bit, from one side to the other (as if you were rolling up a poster). When the dough has been rolled up, allow it to rest for 1 hour.

After the dough has risen, coil it loosely, so that it resembles a snail shell. Transfer the coil to a greased baking sheet. Cover with an extremely large inverted bowl or bucket, large enough to ensure that the dough will not stick to the bowl's surface when it rises. Allow the dough to rise for several hours.

Preheat the oven to 375°F (190°C). Bake the dough coil for around 45 minutes, or until the top is golden-brown. Brush the surface with melted butter and sprinkle generously with sugar. To serve, cut into slices.

Ingredients

4 tsp dried yeast
8 fl. oz milk, warmed
4 oz sugar
1 tsp salt
16 oz all-purpose flour
2 large eggs
2 tbsp olive oil
all-purpose flour, for coating
6 oz butter, softened
butter, for brushing
sugar, for dusting

Serves 8

Granizado
Iced lemonade sorbet

Ingredients
5 juicy lemons
1 pint boiling water
6 oz sugar
1 pint cold water
10 glasses ice slush

Serves 10

*S*itting out under the trees at night, waiting for the first breath of cool air after a long, hot day, nothing is as refreshing as a lemon or coffee granizado.

Wash the lemons and pare the zest from them with a potato peeler. Halve them, squeeze out the juice, and reserve it. Put the zest in a bowl and pour the boiling water over it. Leave until cold.

Remove the zest and stir in the sugar and lemon juice. Let stand for 5 minutes, then stir again, checking that the sugar has dissolved. Bottle and chill this lemonade.

To serve, pour the lemonade into a jug and add an equal amount of cold water. Fill tall glasses with ice slush, pour the liquid over it, and drink through straws.

CHAPTER 6

Central and Western Spain

On the map:
LEON
BURGOS
VALLADOLID
Castilla y Leon
SALAMANCA
SEGOVIA
AVILA
MADRID
TOLEDO
CACERES
Extremadura
Castilla La Mancha
ALBACETE
MERIDA

This vast part of Spain takes in the capital Madrid as well as the regions of Castile & Leon, Extremadura, and La Mancha. The people of Castile were responsible for the creation of Spain as a country, spreading their culture and language across the Iberian peninsula. Today this part of the country remains culturally as well as geographically central. The characteristic features of its landscape include sunflowers, olive groves, and windmills. This is where *Don Quixote*—the cornerstone of Spanish literature—was written; where the finest cheese, manchego, is produced; and where the production of saffron and fine wines is based.

A group of windmills in Campo de Criptana, a small town in La Mancha.

Sopa de lentejas, garbanzos y chorizo
Lentil, garbanzo bean, and chorizo soup

*C*horizo is popular throughout Spain and beyond, with its combination of fiery color and spicy flavor making it the best-known Spanish sausage. The finest chorizo is made on the central plateaux, where the cool, dry air helps in the curing process.

Put the lentils in a large saucepan, pour in enough boiling water to cover them generously, and simmer for about 20 minutes, until just tender. Drain well.

Heat the oil in the rinsed-out saucepan and gently fry the chorizo, onion, and garlic for 4 minutes. Stir in the cumin, coriander, cinnamon, and chile, followed by the tomatoes, garbanzo beans, tomato paste, and stock. Bring to a boil, reduce the heat, cover, and simmer for 15 minutes. Add salt and pepper and lemon juice to taste. Ladle the soup into bowls and serve.

Ingredients
4 oz brown or green lentils
2 tbsp olive oil
2 oz chorizo, chopped
1 onion, finely chopped
2 garlic cloves, crushed
3 tsp ground cumin
2 tsp ground coriander
½ tsp ground cinnamon
¼ tsp crushed dried chile pepper
4 tomatoes, peeled, seeded, and chopped
14-oz can garbanzo beans, rinsed and drained
1 tbsp tomato paste
2 pints vegetable or chicken stock
salt and ground black pepper
juice of ½ lemon, to taste

Serves 4

Ensalada San Isidro
Saint Isidore mixed salad from Madrid

*T*his salad traditionally opens the meal eaten during the festival of Saint Isidore the Laborer, patron saint of Madrid. The joyous celebrations occur in the middle of May, marking the death of the saint who has been associated with peasants and farmers for over a thousand years.

First make the vinaigrette. Mash the garlic on a board with a pinch of salt, working with the flat of a knife or in a mortar. In a bowl or the mortar, stir in the vinegar, paprika, and pepper, followed by the olive oil.

Soak the onion rings in water for 10 minutes, then drain and blot dry with paper towel. This helps remove the acrid aftertaste of strong onions.

Line the base of a shallow salad bowl or platter with lettuce. Flake the tuna over it, then decorate with the onion rings, sliced cooked eggs, cucumber, and olives. Add the slices of tomato and the canned asparagus, if using.

Sprinkle with some of the vinaigrette.

Ingredients

1 garlic clove, finely chopped
¼ tsp salt
3 tbsp sherry vinegar
pinch of paprika
freshly ground black pepper
3½ fl. oz olive oil
1 lettuce, washed and dried
7-oz can tuna, drained
1 onion, peeled and sliced into rings
2 hard-cooked eggs, peeled and sliced
½ cucumber, cut into chunks
6 tbsp small olives
2 tomatoes, sliced
9-oz can white asparagus, drained (optional)

Serves 4–6

Manchego al ajo y estragón
Manchego with garlic marinade and tarragon

*M*anchego is the glory of Spanish cheesemaking—milky and mild, with a slightly salty flavor and a very firm texture. Don't remove the rind before marinating.

Cut the cheese into small chunks and put in a jar or porcelain pot. Stir the vinegar into the olive oil and pour over the cheese. Chop the tarragon leaves finely. Crush the garlic clove and a few peppercorns. Sprinkle tarragon, garlic, and pepper over the cheese. Mix everything well with clean hands.

Seal the jar or pot and leave for 4 days before eating.

Ingredients
1 lb manchego cheese
2 tsp white wine vinegar
¼ pint olive oil
½ oz bunch tarragon
1 clove garlic
black peppercorns

Serves 4–6 as a tapa

Pisto manchego
Stewed vegetables

Ingredients

2 large onions, thinly sliced
2 oz raw ham or bacon, cubed (optional)
3 tbsp olive oil
3 garlic cloves, finely chopped
3 green bell peppers, seeded and chopped
5 large ripe tomatoes, skinned and seeded
3 zucchini, sliced
salt and freshly ground black pepper
pinch of ground nutmeg
4 tbsp chopped fresh parsley
4–8 eggs

Serves 4

Although best eaten hot with poached eggs, this mixture is also excellent served cold, with the eggs scrambled in and a little olive oil poured over. It is always worth making double the amount of pisto, if you have time, because it makes a very good sauce for meat. It will keep in an airtight container for 2–3 days in the fridge.

Fry the onions (and ham or bacon, if using) gently in the oil, adding the garlic toward the end. Add the peppers and fry for 5 minutes. Add the tomatoes and zucchini and cook over low heat, stirring occasionally, until the tomatoes reduce. Season well, adding the nutmeg and parsley.

The eggs may be broken into nests made in the mixture and lightly poached, or they may be scrambled in; or poach them separately and serve alongside the vegetables. The pisto may also be baked in a dish with the eggs in nests, which takes about 10 minutes in a hot oven (375°F/190°C).

Paella de verduras con pesto de nueces
Vegetable paella with walnut pesto

*T*he combination of earthy walnut pesto with delicate, saffron-infused rice is simply magical. Chopped walnuts can be sprinkled on top of the paella to further enhance the nutty flavor of the rice.

First, make the walnut pesto. Place the basil leaves, chopped walnuts, grated cheese, and garlic in a food processor and blend until a paste forms. With the motor still running, add the olive oil and walnut oil little by little, until well incorporated. Set the pesto aside.

Combine the chicken broth, white wine, and saffron in a skillet over low heat. Keep heated until ready for use.

To make the paella, heat the olive oil in a paella pan and sauté the onion and pepper over medium heat for several minutes. Mix in the mushrooms, zucchini, tomatoes, artichokes, parsley, and paprika, and cook for several minutes longer.

Pour in the rice, and combine well. Stir in the broth mixture and pesto sauce and continue to cook until the liquid has been absorbed and the rice is tender. Serve warm and, if desired, sprinkled with chopped walnuts.

Ingredients

2 oz fresh basil leaves, finely chopped
3 tbsp chopped walnuts
3 tbsp grated Manchego or Parmesan cheese
4 cloves garlic, finely chopped
4 tbsp olive oil
2 tbsp walnut oil
1 pint chicken broth
¾ cup dry white wine
½ tsp saffron
4 tbsp olive oil
1 small onion, finely chopped
1 medium red bell pepper, finely chopped
4 oz oyster mushrooms, destemmed and chopped
4 oz shiitake mushrooms, destemmed and chopped
2 zucchini, chopped
2 tomatoes, finely chopped
8 artichoke hearts, quartered
2 tbsp chopped parsley
½ tsp sweet paprika
12 oz paella rice
chopped walnuts, to garnish (optional)

Serves 6

Paella Extremeña
Extremaduran paella

Ingredients

6 fl. oz olive oil
8 oz pork loin, cleaned and diced
8 oz skinless, boneless chicken breasts, diced
2 medium onions, chopped
5 cloves garlic, finely chopped
8 oz chorizo, case removed and crumbled or sliced
2 green bell peppers, cut into thin strips
2 large tomatoes, skinned, seeded, and chopped
1 lb rice
2 pints beef broth
1 tsp turmeric
¼ tsp saffron
¼ tsp dried oregano
pinch of dried thyme
salt and freshly ground pepper, to taste
8 oz Serrano ham, chopped

Serves 8

*A*lthough critics have dismissed the cuisine of Spain's arid Extremadura region as mere "country cooking," it is slowly gaining popularity among those who appreciate basic, unadorned fare. Relying primarily on pork, ham, lamb, and potatoes, recipes from Extremadura tend to be simple, yet immensely satisfying. This very filling paella, influenced by Extremaduran cuisine, features generous portions of Serrano ham, pork loin, chicken, and chorizo (the delectable Spanish sausage which, some speculate, originated in Extremadura).

Heat half of the olive oil in a paella pan over medium heat. Add the pork and cook until done, about 10 minutes. Transfer to a different pan and set aside.

Cook the chicken in the paella pan until done, about 10 minutes. Transfer the chicken to the pan containing the pork.

Pour the remaining oil in the paella pan and sauté the onions for 5 minutes. Add the garlic and cook for a further 3 minutes. Add the chorizo sausage and cook for 5 minutes. Stir in the bell peppers and tomatoes and cook for a further 10 minutes over low heat.

Increase the heat to medium, add the rice to the pan, and sauté for 5 minutes. Pour in the broth. Mix in the cooked pork and chicken, and add the turmeric, saffron, oregano, thyme, salt, and pepper. Cook for 15 minutes. Add the ham and cook for a further 7 minutes or until the liquid has been absorbed and the rice is tender.

Albóndigas al azafrán
Meatballs with saffron

*S*paniards love meatballs and eat them often. In La Mancha it seems that saffron goes into every dish, too. The meatballs can be served plain, or with a simple sauce made by chopping, reducing, and seasoning tomatoes.

Crumble the bread by hand or in a food processor, and process or chop the ham or bacon. Mix in all the meat, lemon zest and juice, thyme, salt, and cayenne pepper. Beat the eggs in a cup and stir in the saffron. Pour the eggs into the meatball mixture and combine. Put spoonfuls of this mixture on a floured baking sheet and roll to coat them with flour.

Fry the meatballs in hot oil, shaking the pan now and then so the meatballs roll over and take on a golden color on all sides. Remove from the heat when the meatballs are cooked through. They take about 10 minutes.

Ingredients

2 slices stale bread

4 oz ham or bacon

1 lb ground pork or veal

pinch of finely grated lemon zest

1 tbsp lemon juice

pinch of dried thyme

½ tsp salt

pinch of cayenne pepper

2 large eggs

pinch of powdered saffron

6 tbsp flour

6 tbsp olive oil

Serves 4

Conejo al azafrán
Rabbit with saffron

Ingredients

2 large onions, chopped
7 tbsp olive oil
1 garlic clove, finely chopped
30 saffron strands
2½ lb rabbit, in pieces
salt and freshly ground black pepper
9 fl. oz white wine
15 black peppercorns, lightly crushed
¼ tsp ground cumin
1 tsp paprika
pinch of cayenne pepper
6 sprigs fresh thyme
1 bay leaf

Serves 4

This is a rabbit dish rich with the tastes of La Mancha—highly spiced with thyme and also with cumin, which was introduced by the Arabs a millennium ago when they came to plant saffron.

Fry the onions slowly in 2 tablespoons of oil in a frying pan, adding the garlic as they soften. Powder the saffron strands with your fingers and soak in 4 tablespoons of hot water.

Remove the onion and garlic from the pan and add about 4 tablespoons more oil. Season the rabbit and fry the meaty portions (back legs and saddle) for 10 minutes. Tuck in the thinner pieces and fry for about another 10 minutes until everything is golden. Remove the rabbit and drain off all the oil.

Add the wine and stir to deglaze the pan. Pack the rabbit pieces tightly into an ovenproof dish and add the onion, wine, saffron liquid, crushed peppercorns, cumin, paprika, and cayenne. Tuck in the thyme and the crumbled bay leaf. Add 4 fl. oz water to almost cover the meat. Cover and simmer very gently for about 1 hour until tender, making sure it does not get dry. Taste and add more seasonings. Be as bold as you dare—you're unlikely to season it more than the locals do!

Perdices a la Toledana
Partridges in wine with new potatoes

*S*hooting partridges is a common sport in the hills behind Toledo, *where this dish comes from, and they are trapped all over the country as they fly through on their twice-yearly migration. The birds here are set off beautifully by the piquant wine sauce.*

Choose a heatproof dish into which the birds fit snugly, then season them inside and out with salt and pepper. Fry the birds in the oil, turning them over and propping them against the sides of the pan, until they are colored on all sides. Remove and keep warm.

Fry the onion in the same oil, adding the garlic when it softens. Bed the birds down into the onion. Add the bay leaves, lemon zest, wine, vinegar, and sufficient stock to cover the legs. Simmer, covered, over a low heat for about 15 minutes.

Meanwhile, simmer the potatoes in boiling salted water for 10 minutes. Move to the dish, pushing them into the spaces between the birds. Cook until they are done.

Remove the potatoes and the birds. Halve the partridges and arrange in a warm serving dish. Surround them with the potatoes. Keep warm. Discard the bay leaves and lemon zest and blend the remaining contents of the dish in a blender or food processor. Reheat and check the seasoning. Pour a little of the sauce over the birds and sprinkle with parsley. Pass the remaining sauce round in a pitcher.

Ingredients

3 fat partridges, wishbones removed
salt and freshly ground black pepper
3 tbsp olive oil
1 large onion, chopped
3 garlic cloves, finely chopped
3 bay leaves
1 strip lemon zest
6 fl. oz dry white wine
4 tbsp sherry vinegar
7 fl. oz chicken stock
24 baby new potatoes
chopped fresh parsley

Serves 6

Cochifrito
Fried lamb with lemon juice

Ingredients

1¾ lb tender lamb
salt and freshly ground black pepper
2 tbsp olive oil
1 onion, chopped
2 tsp paprika
2 garlic cloves, finely chopped
9 fl. oz lamb stock or water
juice of 1 lemon
2 tbsp chopped fresh parsley

Serves 6

Castilian lamb is always superb. In restaurants the animal is baked whole in large, domed ovens. At home it is more likely to be fried simply, often with lemon juice.

Trim excess fat from the lamb and cut the meat into strips. Season with salt and pepper. Heat the oil in a large, heavy-based saucepan over your hottest burner. Add the meat and onion and turn constantly with a wooden spoon until the meat is sealed on all sides.

When the meat is golden and the onion is soft, sprinkle with paprika and add the garlic. Cook for a couple more minutes, then pour in the stock or water. Continue cooking over medium heat until the liquid has virtually gone.

Sprinkle with lemon juice and parsley, cover, and simmer for 5 minutes. Check the seasonings before serving.

A shepherd near Cuenca driving his flock home along a country road.

Patatas a la importancía
Potatoes made special

*T*his is an excellent potato dish to precede roast meat, but it also makes a modest supper dish if served with canned salmon flaked over the top.

Turn the potato cubes in well-seasoned flour. Pour oil into a skillet to come ½ inch deep and heat. Flip the potatoes in beaten egg and fry in batches, turning them regularly. Remove to paper towel when they are browned, adding new ones to take their place.

Meanwhile fry the onion in 2 tablespoons of oil in a wide, shallow saucepan, adding the garlic as the onion softens. Add the potatoes, packing them in well. Pour in the wine, dissolve the saffron in the stock, and add to the pan, together with the bay leaf and parsley. Season gently and simmer, covered, for 20 minutes.

Ingredients

4 large potatoes, diced
6 tbsp flour
salt and freshly ground black pepper
plenty of oil for frying
2 large eggs, beaten
1 onion, finely chopped
2 garlic cloves, finely chopped
4 fl. oz dry white wine
pinch powdered saffron
9 fl. oz chicken stock
1 bay leaf
4 tbsp chopped fresh parsley

Serves 4–6

Spanish field workers harvesting potatoes

Lentejas a la perfecta
Perfect lentils

Ingredients

½ lb green lentils

salt

4 garlic cloves, finely chopped

1 thick slice country bread

4 tbsp olive oil

2 tbsp red wine vinegar

Serves 4

*I*n central Spain, lentils are often cooked with pieces of pig—ears, sausages, pork belly, and so on. Cooked plain, as here, they go well with fried sausages, chorizo, or roast pork.

Bring the lentils to a simmer in a large saucepan full of water, adding salt only when they are done—after around 30 minutes.

Meanwhile, fry the garlic and bread in olive oil in a skillet. When golden on both sides, tip the contents of the skillet—including the oil—into a mortar or blender and pulp. Add the vinegar and stir to combine.

Pour off the water in the saucepan, except for a couple of spoonfuls, and stir in the bread paste. Simmer for a minute to allow the flavors to blend.

CHAPTER 7

Andalusia

Andalusia

CÓRDOBA

SEVILLE

GRANADA

ALMERIA

JEREZ

MALAGA

GIBRALTAR

This southern region has been home to numerous successive cultures, most importantly the Moors, whose residence here for many centuries in the Middle Ages has left a clear stamp on the architecture, culture, and gastronomy. The culinary center of Andalusia is Seville, famous for its excellent broiled seafood, the local specialty ham, jamón ibérico, lamb's kidneys in a sherry sauce, and the deliciously refreshing cold soup, gazpacho. Many of these, and other Andalusian dishes, are legacies of the Moorish presence—think, for example, of the deep-fried pastries bathed in honey which are often served as a dessert.

The Alhambra was formerly the residence of the Moorish rulers of Andalusia. Today, its splendid Islamic architecture makes the palace one of the biggest tourist attractions in the country.

Gazpachuelo
Potato and fish soup

The vinegar in this warm soup is the link with gazpacho. It is surprisingly good and easy to make, so in Spain it is associated with emergencies! The idea is to stretch fish for one or two people to make soup for six.

Put the stock or water, potatoes, and salt in a stockpot. Cook until the potatoes are almost tender, then add the fish, cut into small pieces, for the last 5 minutes. Remove the potatoes and fish to a serving bowl.

Let the stock cool a little. Stir the mayonnaise into the stock to make a creamy soup. Pour the soup over the potatoes and fish. Check the seasoning, stir in the vinegar, and serve warm. Sometimes a pitcher of vinegar is passed round at the table.

Ingredients
1 ¼ pints fish stock or water
1 ½ lb new potatoes
½ tsp salt
1–2 small fish (such as red mullet or sole), scaled and filleted
10 fl. oz mayonnaise (homemade if possible)
2 tbsp white wine vinegar

Serves 6

Pimientos asados al ajo
Roasted peppers with garlic

*R*oasting the peppers for this recipe makes them taste deliciously smoky; they are then stewed slowly with a sweet–sour, intensely garlicky sauce, making a wonderful combination of flavors.

Place the peppers in a large, heavy skillet with the sliced garlic and the olive oil. Sprinkle with salt, and cover. Cook gently, covered, for about 20 minutes over very low heat, turning once or twice.

When the peppers are very tender, remove the lid, and increase the heat to medium-high. Add the balsamic vinegar, then remove from the heat and add the white wine vinegar. Pour into a bowl and allow to cool. When cold, add more salt and wine vinegar if wished.

Ingredients

3 each: red and yellow bell peppers, roasted, peeled, and cut into bite-size pieces
15 to 20 cloves garlic, thinly sliced
3½ fl. oz olive oil
salt to taste
balsamic vinegar to taste
white wine vinegar to taste

Serves 4

Pinchitos morunos
Spicy Moorish kabobs

*E*urope's first kabobs were brought by the Arabs from Africa. They are eaten everywhere in Spain as a tapa, though nowadays they are made from pork rather than the original lamb. Spices for them are sold ready-mixed in Andalusia. Curry powder has been used as part of this mixture, as it contains cumin and the identical herbs.

Crush the garlic with the salt in a mortar, then work in the other ingredients. Skewer the pork, 3 or 4 cubes on a small stick, and marinate them in a shallow dish, turning so they are well coated. Leave at least a couple of hours.

Spread the pinchitos out well on a barbecue or on foil under a broiler. Cook them under a high heat for about 3 minutes on each side.

Ingredients

2 garlic cloves, finely chopped
2 tsp salt
1 lb lean pork, cubed
1 tsp mild curry powder
½ tsp coriander seeds
1 tsp paprika
¼ tsp dried thyme
freshly ground black pepper
3 tbsp olive oil
1 tbsp lemon juice

Serves 6 as a tapa

Gazpacho Andaluz
Classic Andalusian gazpacho

*T*his basic version of gazpacho is the one travelers would be most likely to encounter when touring through Spain. The fact that this soup is commonly found, however, in no way renders it "ordinary." One taste of this chilled gazpacho and you will be instantly transported to a land of whitewashed walls, red-tiled roofs, and a golden sun.

Combine the olive oil, vinegar, garlic, salt, cumin, and Tabasco sauce in a food processor with half of the vegetables listed and purée. Transfer the soup mixture to a large bowl. Purée the remaining vegetables and add to the soup. Add ice cubes (or water) to taste, and additional salt if necessary. Refrigerate until very cool, or overnight.

Before serving, garnish the gazpacho with chopped tomatoes, croutons, and hard-cooked eggs.

Ingredients
4 fl. oz olive oil
2 fl. oz red wine vinegar
3 cloves garlic, chopped
1 tbsp salt
¼ tsp ground cumin
⅛ tsp Tabasco sauce
4 large ripe tomatoes, sliced
2 lb canned plum tomatoes
1 green bell pepper, sliced
1 cucumber, sliced
½ onion, sliced
ice cubes

To garnish:
chopped tomatoes
croutons
hard-cooked eggs

Serves 8

Gazpacho verde
Green gazpacho

*T*his colorful variation on the traditional red gazpacho hails from Huelva and the Sierra Morena in Andalusia. Unlike the classic gazpacho recipes, this soup relies on spinach, lettuce, parsley, and mint for its freshness and texture. Although it is quite different from its more traditional gazpacho cousins, this version is every bit as refreshing.

In a blender, combine the lettuce, spinach, scallions, chile, cucumber, and parsley until the mixture forms a purée. Gradually add in the chicken broth, soured cream, mayonnaise, mint, white pepper, and salt. Purée the mixture until it reaches an even consistency. Refrigerate the soup until you are ready to serve.

Serve the soup chilled in individual bowls, with a spoonful of soured cream over each serving, if desired.

Ingredients

4 oz lettuce leaves, chopped

4 oz spinach

3 scallions, diced

½ red chile pepper, seeded and chopped

½ cucumber, peeled and diced

1 tbsp chopped parsley

16 fl. oz chicken broth

4 fl. oz soured cream, plus extra to garnish (optional)

4 fl. oz mayonnaise

1 tsp chopped fresh mint leaves

½ tsp white pepper

½ tsp salt

Serves 4–6

Gazpacho blanco
White gazpacho

*T*his dish is a modern adaptation of Malaga's ajo blanco. Unlike ajo blanco, however, this version omits the almonds and relies on soured cream and yogurt for its unmistakable creamy texture.

In two batches, purée all the ingredients except for the almonds and grapes in a food processor. Combine both batches in a large bowl and refrigerate for several hours or overnight.

Immediately before serving, garnish individual servings with the diced bell pepper and tomatoes and the croutons.

Ingredients
3 medium cucumbers, peeled and chopped
3 cloves garlic, chopped
16 fl. oz soured cream
8 fl. oz plain yogurt
8 fl. oz chicken broth
salt and pepper, to taste
⅛ teaspoon Tabasco sauce

To garnish:
½ green bell pepper, seeded and diced
2 small tomatoes, seeded and diced
croutons

Serves 6

Ajo blanco
Chilled white almond soup

Ingredients

6 oz blanched almonds

4 slices crustless white bread, soaked in cold water for 5 minutes

3 garlic cloves, sliced

5 tbsp olive oil

1 pint cold water

2 tbsp sherry vinegar

salt

3 oz seedless green grapes

toasted slivered almonds

chopped fresh parsley (optional)

Serves 4–6

Ajo blanco, a white version of gazpacho, is believed to have originated with the Moors. If a silkier texture is desired, try soaking the blanched almonds in milk before processing. This will enhance the soup's delicate creaminess.

Combine the almonds, bread, and garlic in a food processor and blend until smooth. With the motor still running, slowly pour in the olive oil until a smooth paste is formed. Add in the cold water and the vinegar. Process until the mixture is thin and smooth. Season with salt to taste.

Pour the mixture into a large bowl. Float the grapes on the top of the soup. Cover and allow to chill in the refrigerator. To serve, pour the soup into individual soup bowls and garnish with the toasted almond slivers and chopped parsley, if desired.

Higaditos de pollo con vinagre de Jerez
Chicken livers with sherry vinegar

*T*he term "sherry" is an anglicization of Jerez—the name of the Andalusian city which is the center of sherry production. The Moors, in the eighth century, introduced the fortification of wine to southern Spain, and sherry was the most notable result. Here it is used to transform chicken livers into a fine, rich dish.

Wash and trim the chicken livers to remove the green bile sacs and any gristle.

Mix the paprika, garlic, salt, and pepper together in a bowl. Toss the livers to cover in the mix.

Heat 2 ounces of the butter in a large skillet. Cook the livers over high heat in the butter, stirring continuously, until sealed and browned all over. Place livers in a warmed bowl.

Add the onion to the pan and soften over a lower heat. Turn up the heat again, add the vinegar and sugar, and cook until the vinegar is almost dry. Add the broth, stir, and reduce to half the quantity.

Take the remaining butter, break into small pieces, and stir until it melts into the liquid. Check the seasoning and pour the sauce over the livers. Serve in a large bowl or in smaller, individual ones.

Ingredients
1 lb chicken livers
1 tsp paprika
1 tsp garlic
½ tsp each salt and freshly ground black pepper
4 oz butter
½ onion, finely chopped
2 fl. oz sherry vinegar
1 tsp sugar
½ pint chicken broth
2 oz butter

Serves 4

Sherry barrels in a cellar in Jerez.

Riñones en salsa de Jerez
Kidneys in sherry sauce

Ingredients

1½ lb lamb or veal kidneys

6 fl. oz olive oil

2 tsp garlic, crushed

1 tsp paprika

2 onions, chopped

3½ fl. oz sherry

½ pint chicken broth

salt and freshly ground
   black pepper

fresh thyme sprigs

Serves 4

*L*amb and veal kidneys are tender and flavorful. Avoid overcooking them, as this can make them unpleasantly tough.

Clean the kidneys, removing the hard core and any fat. Slice thinly with a sharp knife.

Bring a pan of water to a boil and plunge the kidneys in for one minute to remove the bitterness.

Heat the oil and fry half the kidneys, with 1 teaspoon of the garlic and ½ teaspoon of the paprika. Cook quickly, stirring so that the garlic does not burn. When cooked, blend in a food processor. Keep to one side.

In the same pan, cook the onions until soft. Place the remaining kidneys in the pan with the other teaspoon of garlic and ½ teaspoon of paprika, and the sherry and broth. Bring to a boil.

Lower the heat, add the puréed kidneys, stir, and simmer until the whole kidneys are tender (approximately 5 minutes). Season and serve garnished with sprigs of thyme.

Paella de picadillo
Paella with picadillo

*T*his Andalusian-inspired paella incorporates picadillo, a light dish served throughout southern Spain during the summer. Traditionally a mixture of oil, bell peppers, onions, garlic, tomato, and meat (typically chicken or beef), picadillo is widely popular throughout Andalusia and takes only minutes to prepare. Here, picadillo is deliciously paired with paella, creating a more filling main-course meal. This works well as a refreshing lunch or an informal dinner.

Add the raisins to the warmed sherry and set aside. Cook the sausage, ground beef, chorizo, onion, and garlic over medium heat until the meat is cooked and browned. Drain the fat. Stir in the raisins and sherry, the undrained tomatoes, the chiles, sugar, cinnamon, cumin, and cloves. Bring to a boil, reduce the heat, and cook, uncovered, for 30 minutes or until almost all the liquid has evaporated, stirring occasionally.

Heat the olive oil in a paella pan. Add the rice and sauté for 5 minutes. Pour in the broth and saffron and cook for 20 minutes. Add the sausage mixture, stir, and cook for a further 5 minutes or until the rice is tender and the liquid has been absorbed. Serve immediately.

Ingredients

2½ oz raisins
2 fl. oz dry sherry, warmed
8 oz pork sausage
8 oz lean ground beef
4 oz chorizo sausage
1 onion, peeled and chopped
3 cloves garlic, minced
14-oz can diced tomatoes
4 oz mild green canned chiles, drained, diced
2 tbsp sugar
1 tsp ground cinnamon
¼ tsp ground cumin
⅛ tsp ground cloves
2 tbsp olive oil
12 oz rice
1½ pints beef broth
¼ tsp saffron

Serves 6

Pato a la Sevillana
Duck with oranges and olive, Seville style

Ingredients

1 oven-ready duck
salt and freshly ground black pepper
2 tbsp olive oil
1 onion, finely chopped
1 green bell pepper, seeded and chopped
1 large tomato, skinned, seeded, and chopped
1 tbsp flour
7 fl. oz fino sherry
1 Seville orange (or 1 sweet orange plus
 ½ lemon)
1 bay leaf
8–10 parsley stalks, bruised
5–10 fl. oz duck or chicken stock
2 large carrots
5 oz green olives

Serves 4

*T*he original "duck with orange" comes from the city that introduced bitter oranges to Europe in the eleventh century. Their sharp juice and the salty olives make the duck seem fatless. Since it is a party dish, an elegant modern presentation is given here.

Quarter the duck, removing the backbone, visible fat, and hanging skin. Season and prick the remaining skin well. Heat the oil in a large, heavy-based saucepan and brown the duck on all sides.

Remove the duck and all but 2 tablespoons of fat from the saucepan. Fry the onion in this fat until soft, adding the pepper and tomato halfway through. Sprinkle with flour and stir in. Add the sherry and stir until simmering.

Fit the duck pieces back into the saucepan compactly, tucking in the backbone and 2 strips of thinly pared orange zest. Slice the orange (and lemon, if using) without peeling it, and tuck the slices round the duck, pushing in the bay leaf and parsley stalks. Add enough stock to almost cover, and simmer with the lid on for 45 minutes.

Quarter the carrots lengthwise, remove the cores, and cut them into olive-sized lengths. In a separate saucepan, simmer them in boiling water for 5 minutes.

Remove the duck pieces and discard the backbone, parsley stalks, orange zest, and bay leaf. Purée the sauce through a vegetable mill or blender. Reurn the duck to the saucepan and pour in the sauce. Add the olives and carrot pieces and simmer for another 10 minutes or until the carrots are tender.

Move the duck pieces to a serving dish with a slotted spoon. Surround with the carrots and olives and keep warm. If there is too much sauce, boil to reduce it a little. Any floating fat can be removed by pulling strips of paper towel across the surface. Check the seasonings, pour the sauce over the duck, and serve.

Habas a la rondeña
Broad beans with ham, Ronda style

*I*n Spain this dish is made with raw Serrano ham, which is why it
is known as "Ronda style" even though it is eaten everywhere—
*the sierras of Ronda are famous for their hams from the black-footed
pig. In summer, when parsley is difficult to find in the south, the
garnish may be diced red bell pepper or tomato.*

Fry the onion in the oil in a large, heavy-based saucepan. As it starts to soften, add the
ham and garlic and fry until lightly browned. Stir in the beans (frozen beans need no
water fresh ones need 4 fl. oz). Cover and simmer until tender, stirring occasionally.
Fresh or frozen, they take about 10 minutes.

Season the beans generously, stir in the chopped eggs, and heat through. Stir in the
parsley and serve.

Ingredients
6 oz onion, chopped
4 tbsp olive oil
6 oz raw ham
1 garlic clove, finely chopped
2 lb young podded (or frozen) broad beans
salt and freshly ground black pepper
4 hard-cooked eggs, peeled and chopped
2 oz fresh parsley, chopped

Serves 6

Helado de pasas de Málaga
Málaga raisin ice cream

Ingredients
4 oz muscatel raisins
vanilla ice cream to serve 4
9 fl. oz Málaga wine or sweet
   oloroso sherry

Serves 4

*I*ce cream is very popular in the south of Spain, but rarely made at home. This rich, sweet dessert is based on store-bought vanilla ice cream—but few mass-produced varieties have the kind of elegant flavor which you can obtain by adding raisins and sweet wine.

Pour about 4 tablespoons of boiling water over the raisins and leave to soak for 2 hours. Drain and fold them into the vanilla ice cream, then spoon into 4 bowls. Pour the wine or sherry over and serve.

Index

Picture credits

The images in this book are used with the permission of the copyright holders stated below. (Images are listed by page number.) All other illustrations and pictures are © Quintet Publishing Limited. While every effort had been made to credit contributors, Quintet Publishing would like to apologize should there have been any omissions or errors, and would be pleased to make the appropriate correction for future editions of this book.